MY WAR

THE TRUE EXPERIENCES OF A U.S. ARMY AIR FORCE PILOT IN WORLD WAR II

by

JOHN C. WALTER

authorHOUSE

1663 LIBERTY DRIVE, SUITE 200
BLOOMINGTON, INDIANA 47403
(800) 839-8640
www.authorhouse.com

First published by AuthorHouse 08/02/04

ISBN: 1-4184-4725-0 (sc)
ISBN: 1-4184-4726-9 (dj)

Library of Congress Control Number:2004094227

Printed in the United States of America
Bloomington, Indiana

This book is printed on acid-free paper.

DEDICATED TO

BILL NOLAND
TOM SEVALD
NELSON KURZ

THEY GAVE EVERYTHING

I GAVE A LITTLE TIME

TABLE OF CONTENTS

FOREWORD

There may be a few persons interested in reading about what I did in World War II. If so, that's great, if not, I wrote it anyway. I just thought that I ought to chronicle the memories of my participation. Sometime, someone might just be interested.

Over sixty years have passed since I began active participation in the urban renewal program the Allies organized for Hitler's Germany. The uniqueness of that experience is undoubtedly the reason why the passage of so many years has not dimmed many of the memories. Time, however, has been kind and softened but not diminished the senseless reality of the unpleasant ones.

Helping my recall are the letters I wrote to the folks and Barbara during those experiences. Thoughtfully, Mother and Barbara saved those letters. Also, helping in this recall are the bomb fuse safety tags that John Ingleman, our Bombardier, gave us after each mission. I used them to document, briefly, some of the details of each mission.

Those looking for literary excellence herein will find this account less than perfect. This is the result of: over use of the pronoun "I"; the disorderly mixing of past and present tenses and the use of certain four letter Anglo-Saxon words.

In defense of these failings, these excuses are offered. It is my story, told first hand; therefore, "I" play a major role. While all of this account deals with the past, some events, on recall, come alive. On occasion, a single four letter word carries more meaning that a paragraph of well composed prose.

I sincerely hope you enjoy it.

September, 2003 —JCW

SECOND LIEUTENANT JOHN C. WALTER
JANUARY 1944

CHAPTER 1
INTRODUCTION

When the Japs decided to help Hitler conquer the World, I was living in Long Beach, California with my sister, Eleanor, and her husband, Gerry Ehmann. I was in my third semester at Long Beach Junior College.

The first I knew of the attack upon Pearl Harbor was when Eleanor awoke me around noon on Sunday, December 7, 1941, to deliver the news. To explain why I was still in bed at noon — The night before Rod, my best friend Bruce Ogilby's brother, had invited Bruce and me to a party at his UCLA fraternity house. It had been a long and joyous night which definitely required some extra recovery time the next morning. Let it be said that the news Eleanor gave me was very sobering. — Literally.

Although the Pearl Harbor attack was a shock, there had been subtle signs that something big was about to happen. For instance, on the preceding Friday afternoon, as Bruce and I had come home from school, our route had taken us by the Long Beach airport and the adjoining Douglas aircraft factory. We were amazed by the feverish nature of the military activity, especially around the Douglas plant. Soldiers were busily setting up antiaircraft guns, putting up telephone poles and stringing phone lines all over the place. Bruce and I both wondered out loud about what was going on. Little did we know

1

then what was about to happen. Apparently the Military either knew or strongly suspected something.

At L.B.J.C. I was currently majoring in History. The first semester had been spent in pre-engineering. However, it soon became apparent that that course of study infringed quite a bit upon my football playing, beach visiting, mountain going and hunting activities. The demand of these more important endeavors meant that less than the necessary study time was being devoted to the curriculum. These conflicts brought about both my exit from engineering studies and my first exposure to what is now called plea bargaining. Dr. Geer, the physics prof, told me if I would change from a pre-engineering to a liberal arts or some other course of study, he would give me a "D" in physics. My decision to continue in engineering would result in a big "F". After considerable thought (all of about 2 seconds worth), the study of history became very attractive and I departed, for a while, from the study of engineering. I completed my fourth semester in June, 1942. However, the credits of my assorted studies did not add in a manner which would qualify me to receive an Associate of Arts degree.

As school ended, it became apparent that the disagreements going on overseas were not to be settled in the very near future. Also, it was becoming obvious Uncle Sam would soon offer me a personal invitation to participate in his military activities. Thus, when school was out, I thought it might be a good idea to make a visit home to Washington, Indiana.

I was over 21 so it was no longer possible for Dad to get a pass for me to make the trip by train. However, now, I was the proud owner of a 1935 Plymouth 4 door sedan. It had been purchased for the staggering (at the time and for my financial status) sum of $105. Gerry's mechanic had gone over it and assured me it was in good shape in spite of some 65,000 miles. The tires were "so-so". This tire situation would turn out to be a real problem later on when tire rationing was put into effect. My employment status did not qualify for either tire replacement and/or the recapping of my tires.

Since "wheels" were available, it was quite logical for me to drive home for the visit. However, I did not really relish making the long drive by myself. In stepped one of my good friends, Lee Craig, a rare native Californian. As such, he had never been out of the state of California. So, I enticed him to go with me, see some of the rest of the country and share the expense and the driving. His two conditions were: he not spend over $60.00 and be gone no more than 2 weeks. The time limit was brought about by the fact that Lee's Draft Board was breathing down his neck. A situation which was somewhat less than comfortable.

To illustrate the consequences of having "so-so" tires on "Betsy" are the following excepts from a letter written to the folks describing our return to Long Beach.

"...on the way into Tulsa, the left rear tire began to go down slowly so we had it fixed - (a series of small [rot] holes along one seam on the inside diameter of the tube).

"[near]...Albuquerque the same tire began to go down again, so we stopped and found it was another 'rot' hole. I decided that was too much, so, I had the tubes from the left rear and the spare switched. This solved the trouble...

"Coming thru the mountains near Williams [Arizona] Lee was driving and he thumped into a chuck hole and I heard the rims clunk. We stopped [made an] inspection [and saw] no apparent damage. ...about 15 miles from Kingman [Arizona] Lee...noticed the car swerving so we stopped and found the left rear tire going down rapidly. ...Changed to the doubtful spare and eased ourselves into Kingman. In Kingman I had the tubes switched again...one patched...the spare casing put on the left rear. The one which had hit the [chuck] hole had a 3 in. cut in it — thru the fabric and all, so I had a boot put in it."

For those mystified by the words "tube", "casing" and "boot", the casing is the outer portion of the tire which carries the tread and

3

fastens to the wheel; the tube fits into the casing and is the thing that holds the air; a boot is a curved piece of rubber coated fabric about twice the size of a man's palm which fits on the inside of the casing to cover up a cut or a hole. It is held in place by the air pressure in the tube pressing it against the casing.

Tubeless tires were in use on bicycles at that time. However, they had not been developed for use on automobiles when Lee and I made our cross country trek.

CHAPTER 2
JOINING UP

Soon after we got back, Uncle Sam grabbed Lee to lend a hand. Out of curiosity, I decided to check with the Draft Board to see how soon my number might come up. Big Surprise!! About August 3rd. I didn't relish being in the walking Army, so I rushed down to the Long Beach Army Recruiting Station to see about joining the Army Air Force. As eyesight is very important to an aviator, they gave me a vision screening test. To my amazement, I flunked it. They said I had 20/30; not the required 20/20.

Since it now looked like I was going to be in the walking Army, I reasoned it would be better to do it as an officer. Therefore, I decided to apply for OCS (Officers' Candidate School). I got the required letters of recommendation and college transcript together and sent them in. Much to my dismay, it turned out the college credits I had were not what they wanted. So much for a miscellaneous major.

I wanted nothing to do with the Navy. While surfing was fun, I felt the Navy over did the water thing. This left two choices as to how to enter the Army: JUMP OR BE PUSHED. Better to jump since this might give me some choice as to what role I would play in the conflict. The Corp of Engineers or the Tank Corps had the most appeal. I told the Sergeant to start signing me up for the walking Army. Which he did. My plan was to get in and then request a transfer to OCS. After I took care of enlistment preliminaries in Long Beach, the next step was to travel to the Los Angeles Army Recruiting Station for the physical exam.

While I was taking the physical, the doctor said I had a good pair of eyes. This was a big surprise. I told him when the Air Force examined me they didn't think so. Now, it was his turn to be surprised.

I told the people in charge to put the walking Army enlistment on hold. I had to have another opinion on this eye business.

A visit to L.A. and Aunt Miriam's eye doctor, Dr. Fuog, to obtain his opinion was my next order of business. He said my problem was called "lazy eye". Since the right eye was better than 20/20 I just wasn't using the left one. He said this could be fixed with a couple of weeks of eye exercises. I told him to sign me up for the program right then and there.

By now, the Draft Board was really on my tail. However, after I described my efforts to join the Air Corps, they granted a deferment until the end of August.

The eye exercises were finished. I passed the eye test given by the Long Beach Air Corps Recruiters and convinced them to let me go to L.A. and take the Aviation Cadet mental and physical exams. The mental exam came first. It was really very easy, consisting of 150 multiple choice questions.

Sample: "Barracks are:
A airplane hangers
B flat-bottomed boats
C living quarters
D street obstructions
E underground passages"

A real "toughie".

Before the test started, the administering officer said only about 55% of us would pass. As it turned out, little less than 42% of the 60 taking the test passed. I was one of the 42%.

The next day I went for the physical. Again, I flunked. This time the eyes were O.K., but my pulse (at 100) was too high. They told me to come back in a week for a recheck.

On my return to Long Beach, I sought out another doctor, Dr. Swinney, a Long Beach heart specialist. He told me nothing was wrong with the "ticker" except that I was probably too excited when the Army doctors checked me. He said the problem could be fixed with a few pills. These (for $1.55) he gave me. Over the following week, I popped the pills and went back to the Los Angeles recruiting station for the recheck.

The entrance exams were given in the Pacific Electric Station at 6th and Main in downtown L.A., the same place used by the walking Army. On the P.E. (interurban) ride to L.A., I found I still had a couple of pills left. So, these went down the hatch. The "If some is good, more is better" theory at work. It was now or never.

The P.E., not unusually, was late getting to L.A. There was no time to wait for the elevator. Time had to be saved by running up the stairs to the third floor. Maybe they'd be behind schedule so I could catch my breath and let the pulse rate settle some before they checked the ticker. No luck. Just as fate would have it, I was called before I even had time to sit down. Pulse rate 76. Doctor's comment: "You sure must have been excited when you were in here last week." The response, between gasps for breath, was: "Sure was!".

I was somewhat surprised he didn't think the combination of a sweaty brow, shortness of breath and a slow heart rate a medical oddity. (After I had been in the Military a little while, his action became perfectly understandable. His job was to check the heart. Breathing and sweating were someone else's area of responsibility.)

This time, I was directed into a big room, told to hold up my right hand, repeat the oath and become U.S. Army Aviation Cadet, serial number 19130275. It was August 18, 1942. It had not been easy, but I had beaten the Draft Board to the punch!

However, all of the Cadet training facilities were full for the next few months. They told me to go home, that they would call when space was available.

When school had ended in May, I had gone to work as a common laborer on a housing project in the L.A. Harbor area. As it could be some time before I was called up, I returned to this job. In order to qualify for this job, it had been necessary for me to join my first union. I became, naturally after paying the dues, a temporary member of the International Hod Carriers, Building and Common Laborers Union of America.

About 6 weeks after enlisting, I was "lured" away from my laborer's job to take a better paying job as a carpenter. Naturally, this meant I had to join another union. I was now also a temporary member of the Carpenters and Jointers of America. My job title was not "Carpenter" but "Pile Butt". (In case there exists some curiosity about the derivation of this job title: After a wooden piling is driven to the required depth in the ground, the excess, or the pile butt, is sawn off.) In this job I worked around the Terminal Island Navy Base in the Los Angeles harbor.

There may be some who doubt that my inherent abilities were adequate for such a skilled job as this. Thus, let it be known that, by some very unusual coincidence, the foreman who hired me also happened to be the father of my girl friend, Billie Stanke. I guess that it was possible for this association to have compensated for my deficiency in both ability and experience as a carpenter.

The months rolled by. While waiting, I also became an Air Raid Warden —- completely outfitted with tin hat, whistle, arm band, flashlight, and a very smelly gas mask. There were drills and brownouts. Brownouts affected all coastal areas. This meant the elimination of all nonessential outside lights, the covering of windows with opaque curtains and the dimming of all street lights. Except, those street lights right along the ocean front. They were turned off completely. Only the car's parking lights could be used when driving at night.

THEN, ONE NIGHT IT HAPPENED!! ATTACK!! The Japs were coming to bomb the Douglas Aircraft Plant just two short miles from us. Searchlights searched. Antiaircraft guns blazed away and the shrapnel fell like steel hail. Our defense held! Not a bomb fell. There were those who held that the little bastards were nowhere near.

Personally, I didn't see them but then who is going to stand outside looking up when shrapnel is falling all around the place? Not this kid!

CHAPTER 3
CALLED UP AND PREFLIGHT

Thanksgiving and Christmas, 1942, came and passed. Soon it was 1943. On February 19th, (what a birthday present!) the long awaited message came. "Report to the Santa Ana California Army Air Base for active duty. Do not bring any civilian clothing except that being worn." THIS WAS IT!! I quit my job and gathered up all my loose junk and took it to Bekins, the moving company warehouse, to be stored for the duration. My car, since I could not take it to Santa Ana, I placed in storage.

However, it turned out to be a very short storage period. While waiting for the bus to take me to Santa Ana, Billie and I got preoccupied, and I missed the bus. This was the last one which could get me there before the reporting time deadline. Now, the only solution was to get my car out of storage and have someone drive me there. The big catch to that solution was that Billie didn't have her driver's license. I went looking for Eleanor but couldn't find her. After some more searching, we found Billie's older sister, Bette, to drive me to Santa Ana. Nothing like getting off to a good start. The date was February 23, 1943.

The reception at Santa Ana was not what could be called cheery. This blended right in with the weather which was cold and rainy.

Since the base was still fairly new, parts of the grounds were very muddy.

The people in charge viewed the newcomers in a somewhat offhanded manner. Just as if we were so much very raw material for their highly tuned Aviation Cadet machine. Which, in fact, we were. They told us that we were members of Class 44A. This meant that, if we did not wash out along the way, we would graduate 10 months later in January, 1944.

In spite of the staff's appearance of not caring, we were given a form letter and told to sign it and address the envelope to our folks. The letter told the folks where we were. The base commanders must have known about kids and letter writing.

Santa Ana was the first of the four steps in the Aviation Cadet Pilot Training program. It was the only one that did not involve flying. The other steps, in order, were Primary, Basic and Advanced Flight Training. This, the first step, would be the longest at about three months. The time spent at Santa Ana involved two phases. The first, Classification, was an indoctrination/classification operation. In this they taught you some basic Army stuff such as, military courtesy, bed making and marching.

For those of us who smoked (I did) we were taught a very important piece of Army etiquette — "field stripping" of cigarette butts. In the Army, to properly dispose of a cigarette butt: first, the paper must be removed, the unburned tobacco crumbled and scattered to the wind and finally the paper compressed into a tiny ball and discretely discarded. Fortunately for us, filter tipped cigarettes were still in the distant future.

We were also run through a series of tests, both physical (reactions) and mental to see where we could be used best.

The second phase, Preflight, was nine weeks of "book learning" relating to the field for which the Cadet had been classified.

Primary, Basic and Advanced Flight Training were each nine weeks long. At any given time, there were at least two classes at each school. This, in typical Military Academy tradition, provided for at least one "upper" and one "lower" class.

I'm sure, if those in charge had been asked, they would have preferred to have four classes on hand at all times. This would have provided three upper classes to hassle one lower class. However, with two classes present, there was always one class available to haze the newcomers. We had our first taste of this class system when, still in civilian clothes, we were marched (herded would be a more correct term) from the reception hall to our barracks. Since we were moving in one bunch, we, at least in our own minds, thought we were marching. We were to learn differently later.

As we moved down the street between the barracks, the upper class proceeded to demonstrate their superior knowledge, experience and training. After all, they were "veterans" of almost six weeks. Given this superiority they felt qualified and certainly duty bound to critique our "formation" with such comments as:

"Look at the head on that one!"

"Shorty, why are you walking in that hole?"

"Hey, this bunch really looks like the bottom of the barrel."

We were destined to hear much more from this bunch of Cadets until it became our turn to be SUPERIOR. We remembered these phrases and invented a few new ones.

Quarters assigned; the next step was to erase the civilian look. The first of a series of operations to accomplish this objective was to eliminate individualism created by dissimilar clothing. So, it was time to get in formation and march off to the Quartermaster (not the clothing store or warehouse). It had become apparent the only place we could go by ourselves was to bed or to the toilet. Anywhere else, it was to be marching, as a group, in formation.

While it is often said the Army has only two sizes of clothes, too big and too small, we did not fare too badly. The clothing was new and clean and fit fairly well.

We were now beginning to all look alike. One big exception. The hair. So, again we got in formation and were marched off to the barber shop. The barbers really had a ball. They would ask each Cadet how he would like his hair cut. The barber, after listening very attentively to the complete set of instructions, would pull out the clippers and make a quick pass either from back to front or front to back. I don't believe any of these barbers owned a comb or a pair of scissors. They really had no need for them. In a jiffy the Cadet's head would look just like the one that preceded. That is, CLIPPED VERY, VERY SHORT.

The hair cutting operation was particularly hard on some of the native born Californians who had been nurturing and cultivating their "ducktails" for many years.

We were still reeling from the trauma of the hair cut when the next shock came. That was the physical exam and the <u>SHOTS</u>. It now was rapidly becoming very apparent that the Army vocabulary does not include the word "modesty". We had suspected that when we saw the toilets in the barracks. Not only they did not have any doors, there were no stalls on which to hang the doors. As we entered the examining room, the order was "Strip to the skin and line up."

It is true that some people faint when they are given a shot. It is also true that some people faint when they THINK they are going to be given a shot. And it is also true that some people faint when they see someone else get a shot. Size and outward appearance of the individual give no clue as to what will happen. Except, the bigger the guy, the bigger the thud when he hits the floor. I didn't "thud". Several did.

As a part of the shot giving operation was another complete physical exam. This almost put me in a state of panic. It had been about six months since I had taken the entrance physical. I wondered, if in the interim, the eyes had reverted to the supposed 20/30 and the heart zoomed back up to 100 bpm. The worry was for naught. I passed without a question.

Being a part of the Army Air Force it was only natural that the place was organized by squadrons and flights. A squadron of 240 men was made up of three flights (A, B and C) of 80 men each. As each barracks held 80 men, it naturally followed that each barracks housed a flight. For Classification I was assigned to Squadron 14; for Preflight it was Squadron 23, A Flight.

We soon found out this business operated six and one half days per week. The big event of the week was the Sunday morning parade. The entire Cadet body was lined up on the parade ground and each unit would pass in parade in front of the base commanding officer and his staff. The real test of this operation was standing at attention while all of the other units passed the reviewing stand. We were warned not to lock our knees while we stood at attention as this was an excellent way to ensure fainting. Apparently some did not heed this advice with the result they prostrated themselves on the parade ground.

Following the regular Sunday morning parade and review, we were allowed the afternoon off. However, "off" in this case did not mean "off of the base" during the first six weeks. Further, to get us used to the military life, we were allowed no visitors for the first 3 weeks.

When the 3 weeks were about up, I managed to get a cold and run a slight fever of 99.8°. This was cause to throw me into the Hospital for four full days. So, I entertained Billie, her sister and brother-in-law from my hospital bed. The medical staff had a real good gimmick going. Once they got a barely sick Cadet inside, they kept him there as long as they could and put him to work as an orderly for the sicker ones. Fortunately, my short hospital stay didn't cause me to fall far enough behind in school I couldn't make it up.

It was now time to begin our formal military training. Our first, in depth instruction, centered upon the bed. We thought we knew well the varied purposes of a bed. We had used them for sleeping, resting, sitting and certain recreational activities. We soon found that the Army had additional and more important uses of the bed. These were: the blanket of a made up bed must be pulled tight enough so that a quarter dropped on the bed would bounce; also the blanket should have its corners folded and tucked in such a manner as to appear as if it had been cut and stitched in place both on top of and underneath the mattress; and most important, there was to be no dust inside the coil springs under the mattress.

The wooden box at the foot of the bed was not a wooden box. That was a footlocker. You don't just throw your junk in it and close the lid. You very carefully arranged your underwear, socks, and toilet articles in the prescribed manner. The end result to be achieved is to make the inside of one footlocker look just like every other one.

Also, when you hung your clothes on the rack, there were rules as to how this was to be done. Saturday morning inspections were a dreaded occurrence. Screw up one of the details and the result would be a "gig" (demerit). Enough gigs and you wound up with one or more "tours" —- a tour was one hour of marching with a rifle on your shoulder during your "free" time.

Now, when it came to moving about outside, the Army had its own system. For instance, when going from point A to point B, if a straight line wouldn't get the job done, you made your way there by a series of straight lines. This may sound simple; however, the practice followed dictated that changing from one straight line to another must be done by a 90° turn either to the left or right. The drill manual did include quarter and half turns, but for some reason or other they were usually only demonstrated on the drill field and the parade ground. This 90° turn business could turn an otherwise simple trip into a circuitous trek.

Before going off on one of these trips we had to get ourselves well organized or "formed up". Here's how that was done. The Squadron Leader, a Cadet that had either been in the Army, ROTC, a military school or knew his right foot from his left, was placed in charge. This person, the Cadet Captain, stood in front of the barracks and blew a police whistle which was the signal for everybody to run out of the barracks and "bunch" up.

It was no surprise to find the Army had very definite ideas as to how this bunching up was done. Four straight lines were to be formed. The spacing between the individuals in the line and between the lines was one arm's length. For some reason this was known as "dressing". Don't ask me why. The tallest guys were at the right end of each of the four lines and the shortest at the left end. I could figure out why this was done. It made the difference in height of the individual Cadets less apparent. This, along with the uniform and the hair cut, combined to further erase or obscure individualism.

Once all of this lining up stuff was accomplished, it was time to move off. The Squadron Leader yelled something that the book said was "Forward March." It sure didn't sound like that but that was what was meant. The Squadron took off with the tall guys in the lead. Always. This resulted in making the short guys in the rear really have to scurry to keep up. Once the group was in motion, there was a lot of fussing about "KEEP IN STEP". The Army severely dislikes to see heads randomly bobbing up and down when the troops march past.

Another of the idiosyncrasies of the Army revealed itself when it came to marching. In civilian life there is the commonly used phrase: "Getting started off on the right foot." Well, when the troops start off, it is on the left foot; not the right one. Never did figure that one out.

We practiced marching quite a lot and consequently became pretty good at it. One Sunday our Flight won the first place award in the Review. For that, the Squadron got its name on a trophy somewhere.

Not unexpectedly, the Army had some very fixed ideas about eating — particularly in regards to when, where, how and how to prepare for it. In spite of all this preoccupation with the eating operation, the place where eating took place was called the Mess Hall. This fact got added to the "Something else I never figured out" list.

Since we were officers-to-be, it was only fitting we not be subjected to the indignity of being served cafeteria style. We were seated at tables and served family style by, whom else but, other Cadets.

The Mess Hall was furnished with two rows of picnic tables. One end of the tables was against the outside wall, thus leaving an aisle down the middle of the room.

The tables were set before the Cadets entered. This chore was performed by Cadets who had been selected for Mess Management, a much more sophisticated term than K.P. After all, we were almost officers. The operation of setting the table was not achieved just by putting plates, utensils, cups, etc. on the table haphazardly. Each element of the table setting was placed in a rigidly prescribed order and fashion which included very precise alignment of all of these elements. The first part of the alignment process was to stretch a string between the ends of the hall. This string was used to make sure the plates, cups, salt shakers, etc. on all of the tables were all in a row from the front to the back of the Mess Hall. After that was accomplished, the string was stretched across the hall to establish alignment in that direction.

Obviously, with all the manpower available, there had to be some activity to absorb it. It was unimportant whether the assigned task was productive or not.

The Cadets entered the Mess Hall by marching, of course. They were directed to their places by commands and were to remain standing at attention until the last man reached his place. Next came the command to be seated but to remain silent and at attention. Finally, the command to eat was given. At that time talking was permitted. While the Cadets were eating, no slouching, or elbows on the table was allowed. Further, there was no reaching across the table. If something was not in reach, you politely asked it be passed. This regimen was new to and hard upon some of the Cadets who had to struggle to learn it.

(If a story that was told is true, this training in politeness was not fool proof. The story goes that a Cadet was invited to have Sunday dinner with a family in Santa Ana. During the course of the meal he is alleged to have politely asked: "Please pass the f——-g butter.") If true, he probably was not asked back.

If the Squadron or an individual had screwed up recently, the order to eat a "square" meal would be meted out as punishment. This meant that during the eating process all movement of the hands and arms must be accomplished by a series of straight vertical or horizontal lines, such as, vertically from the plate to the plane of the mouth and the horizontally into the mouth. Return trip to the plate was in the reverse order. This took concentration and lengthened the time to finish eating which was also tightly regulated. Also talking was not allowed when eating a "square" meal.

The time for eating your meal was rigidly established. If you wolfed your food down, you were not free to get up and leave. You sat there. If you dawdled over your food, you couldn't stay and finish.

The food was not only plentiful, but it was also good. However, at times, there was a screw up, such as when identical bowls were used for the gravy and chocolate syrup. Mashed potatoes with chocolate syrup are not too bad. Vanilla ice cream with gravy is not a real winner. Of course, this mix up should occur only once. The second time could have been a serious enough breech of the regs to lead to washing out, I suspect.

The Army had ways, other than Mess Management, to utilize the wealth of manpower available to them. Two of these were Fire Guard and Mess Hall Guard. In the case of the former, when the Flight was off to school or some other activity, one Cadet was appointed to remain in the barracks as the Fire Guard. He was not to flake out on his bunk for the day but was supposed to patrol both floors of the barracks to detect any incipient fire and sound the appropriate alarm. Also his presence provided, in effect, a security guard. During my stint in the Service, theft was never any problem for me or those around me.

Mess Hall guard duty was of two kinds. Inside and outside. In both cases, the Cadet was armed with an unloaded rifle and no ammunition. As I recall, the duty period was four hours long. I believe the guards were in place from 1800 hours to 0600 hours, thus requiring three shifts per night. The outside guard marched around the place and challenged anyone approaching with evil intent, such as a Cadet in search of an extra serving of ice cream. The inside guard patrolled the kitchen and eating area also looking for snack bandits and watching for the outbreak of fire. Sometimes, the inside guard became confused about his role and switched from guard to snack bandit.

I don't know why we were given rifles for guard duty and tours. We never received a minute's training in the use of rifles. We did get training on the 45 caliber pistol and Thompson machine gun, and we got to try our hand at skeet shooting. It was fun.

In addition to eating, marching, making the bed and "G.I.ing" (cleaning) the barracks, there was school and Phys. Ed. The latter was a full hour and one half of calisthenics every day. Soon found some of my "muscle" wasn't. Also discovered some new muscles. This was tougher than L.B. J.C. football practice had ever been.

On occasion, there were some special barracks activities which were not a part of the regular Cadet program. One of the more memorable ones involved a Cadet by the name of Tullis from Texas. For awhile we accepted the fact that Mr. Tullis had an aversion to taking a shower. We believed that perhaps his idiosyncrasy was due to the fact that in his part of Texas a water shortage existed. After some time, however, this reasoning began to lose its acceptability. We were not now in Texas and water seemed to be fairly plentiful. As the days wore on it became more and more difficult to exist downwind from Mr. Tullis. Finally, a decision was made to eliminate this assault upon our senses of smell. It was time for Mr. Tullis to have a shower, a real good one.

Mr. Tullis was a pretty well muscled Texan so an equally well built party of six was selected to have the honor of showing him how showers were executed. The rest of the barracks stood either in reserve, or as spectators or as door guards. When the coast was clear, out came the G.I. scrub brushes and the G.I. soap, the former coarse and stiff and the latter as strong and caustic as they made. Into the shower went the gallant six and Mr. Tullis. After about 30 minutes of struggle and profanity, Mr. Tullis emerged with a very, very ruddy glow and a new aroma. That was the first and last time it was necessary for others to clean up Mr. Tullis' act.

School was fairly easy. Except for Morse code. The old brain had a tough time converting "dit" and "dah" sounds to "dot" and "dash", respectively, and then trying to translate that baby talk into letters, words and information. The minimum speed for passing the course was 10 words per minute. My score: 10.01 wpm. A close call.

As a part of the screening process, we were "treated" to a ride in the altitude chamber. The altitude chamber was nothing more than a large cylindrical tank laid on its side. Inside, it was equipped with benches to seat 20 cadets plus a Technician. One end of the chamber was equipped with an air lock so entrance and exit, if necessary, could be made without affecting the pressure in the main portion of the chamber.

In operation, the air in the chamber was pumped out to simulate an increase in altitude. The procedure was to lower the pressure at a rate equivalent to an increase in altitude of about 1,500 feet per minute. At the 10,000 feet level oxygen masks were put on for the balance of the "trip" to 38,000 feet. In the trip above 20,000 feet there were several pauses to make sure that everyone had been successful in "clearing" their ears. These pauses were also used to demonstrate the insidious dangers and physical effects associated with the lack of oxygen at these higher altitudes.

One Cadet would "volunteer" to remove his oxygen mask and start writing by copying some printed material. As time went on, the writing became more and more illegible; however the volunteer seemed as happy as a clam. The experiment was ended before the Cadet passed out. When questioned about how he felt as he was writing, his comment was "Fine". A few months later, I would have cause to remember this demonstration.

When a Cadet was "going up" in the chamber, the air (or gas) in the body expanded. If, for instance, this air was trapped in some place such as under a tooth filling, a real humdinger of a toothache could result. Of course, the pressure created by gas trapped in the digestive tract could be relieved in one or both of the two ways possible. The resulting sounds could have been called (altitude) "chamber" music.

Before we knew it, the six weeks were up. We were given our first pass! To a man, at least all of the unmarried ones, this meant the opportunity to bowl over the local female population. When the local damsels failed to swoon at our appearance, we came to the conclusion that Aviation Cadets had been loosed upon this air base territory many, many times before. Thus, we would have to wait until we got to a place where few cadets had been before.

There was one unexpected side benefit. To some of the new non Air Corps enlisted Army personnel we appeared to be officers. At least at a distance. Our green officer's blouse and the garrison cap

THE AUTHOR ON FIRST LEAVE FROM SANTA ANA

with the Cadet insignia (wings with a big propeller) gave all the appearance of an officer. Taking no chances, the enlisted men threw us salutes from across the street and down the block. Naturally, they, in return, received a hand salute that a West Pointer would have found difficult to equal and impossible to beat.

Then came the day. ORDERS HAD BEEN POSTED!! Check the bulletin board!! Although I had been told earlier that I had been classified for Pilot Training, that was no iron clad commitment. Where was I going? Pilot Training, Navigation School, Bombardier School, Gunnery School or oblivion? After searching through the lists on the bulletin board, I found my name on the list scheduled to go to flight training. Hurrah!!

To keep the folks informed, the Colonel sent a letter telling them I had been accepted for Pilot Training and would soon be moving on. So the War Department envelope return address wouldn't scare them, the lower left hand corner of the envelope was stamped "GOOD NEWS". It was sure good news to me!!

CHAPTER 4
PRIMARY FLIGHT SCHOOL

Having been selected for Pilot Training, my next stop was Primary Flight School at Dos Palos, California. It was therefore time to pack up by belongings and cram them into barrack's bag and "enjoy" my first troop train ride. A barrack's bag is a tubular canvas sack about three feet long, eighteen inches in diameter, equipped with a handle and a shoulder strap. When filled with my meager belongings, it could be lifted only by Atlas, and then with considerable effort. How so little could weigh so much and be so unwieldy was a mystery.

The train ride to Dos Palos was uneventful, although it took more than 28 hours to cover the 250 miles from Santa Ana to Dos Palos. Obviously, we spent quite a lot of time standing still and going in the wrong direction. However, on June 23, we arrived in Dos Palos. The train stopped on a siding near a general store, a one pump gas station and a small brown and orange depot. This did not look like a great start.

We had heard Dos Palos was a Country Club. The approximately 250 Cadets on board our train, after looking over the nearby scene, had some very grave doubts at this point.

Soon we were picked up by a tram-like affair and delivered to Dos Palos Army Air Field.

The field had been built by and was operated by civilians. It had been active for almost a year when we arrived. Instead of the WW II two story wooden barracks, our quarters were small clusters of single story cream, trimmed in green, stucco buildings. In the center of each building was a sitting and study room and adjoining bath facilities. On each end of the center room was another room which held 8 beds. Thus, each building had 16 occupants. After Santa Ana this was real luxury. The beds were 3/4 size with inner spring mattresses!! The buildings were air conditioned!! (Almost a necessity for the San Joaquin Valley in the summer time.) We even had a swimming pool!! And there were girls!! And, best of all, there was no mess management or guard duty!!

Despite earlier appearances in the vicinity of the Dos Palos railroad station, this place, indeed, had all the makings of a Country Club. There were some Military around. Not very many. The few included the Commandant of Cadets, Captain Smith, several administrative types and, of course, the dreaded CHECK PILOTS!! Flight and Ground School Instructors, flight line personnel (mostly young girls!!), the mess hall attendants (mostly young girls!!) and the gate guards were all Civilians.

While some of the Military aspects had disappeared, such things as marching, barrack's inspection, parades, and Phys. Ed. continued to be strongly present. Also, it still was not possible to leave the base whenever the whim struck.

For the only time in the whole of my training, the assignment of quarters was not done alphabetically using last names. As a result, I was able to develop friendships with persons whose last names started with letters other then "T", "U", "V", "W", "X", "Y" and "Z".

The food, as it had been at Santa Ana, was good and plentiful. The effect was obvious. When I went to Santa Ana I weighed 154 pounds. Five months later I weighed 180 pounds. The calisthenics had ensured the added weight was not deposited around the waist. My belt size was unchanged.

The pace was hectic. We were up at 4:45 a.m. and went at it hard until 7:30 p.m. It was home work until lights out at 9:00 p.m. That was for 5 days a week. On Saturdays it was inspection and parade in the morning. From then on the rest of the weekend was our own. That is, unless penalty tours needed to be walked off. After the first two weeks we were able to leave the Base between 11:00 a.m. Saturday until 7:00 p.m. Sunday.

Finally, it was time to meet our Flying Instructor and become acquainted with the airplane we were to learn to fly. It was the Ryan PT-22 Recruit, a low wing open cockpit two seat aircraft with an aluminum fuselage and fabric-covered wings and tail. The power was supplied by a Kinner 5 cylinder radial engine which drove a fixed pitch wooden prop. The main landing gear had an extremely wide track with the wheels set well forward. This was a feature we later learned to appreciate. It was almost impossible either to ground loop or nose over this airplane.

Another interesting feature was the number of wires (actually streamlined steel rods) that ran from the top and the bottom of the wings to the top of the fuselage and the landing gear, respectively. We were told that these wires made it practically impossible to pull the wings off of the thing. This feature also made the airplane capable of performing an outside loop, a maneuver few other airplanes can safely perform. The Ryan PT-22 was equipped with landing flaps which the more widely used biplane PT-17 Primary Trainer didn't have.

Now, the time arrived to try it out. The date was June 28, 1943. The first step was to draw a parachute from the Parachute Room. After being issued the chute, it was the Cadet's responsibility to check the parachute log book to make sure that it had been inspected and repacked as prescribed. After struggling into the "jump sack", the sergeant in-charge made sure we knew how to properly adjust all the straps. Using a parachute without the leg straps properly adjusted can be the cause of both immediate severe pain and long lasting suffering. However, after trying a few steps with the straps properly fastened, the Cadet soon realized that it was next to impossible to walk with the leg straps fastened. With the leg straps unfastened, the parachute pack could be pushed up so it rested against your butt, which it bumped with each step. Later, my butt would experience this bumping with more repetition than I really desired.

The design of the PT-22 required the pilot to sit in the rear cockpit when flying solo. This was necessary in order to keep the center of gravity (CG) of the airplane within safe limits. Thus, when the Instructor or a second person was aboard, they sat in the front cockpit. This also resulted in the Cadet always being in the rear cockpit whether flying dual or solo.

Communication between the front and rear cockpits was strictly one way. From Front to Back. A length of rubber tubing ran from the front cockpit to the rear cockpit. At the Instructor's end of the tubing there was a funnel-like instrument with the small end fastened to the tubing. In the rear cockpit the tubing was fastened to a wye connection. Two tubes then ran from the wye connection to two curved metal tubes which were fastened to the ear muffs of the student pilot's helmet. To communicate with the student, the Instructor spoke (most times YELLED) into the funnel. Since all spoken communication was one way, the student could only respond by head or control stick movements. The Instructor could monitor response through a small rear view mirror mounted on his windshield. Some Instructors, on occasion, to impress the student, stuck the funnel into the slip stream. That was a real attention getter!! This system of communication, called a Gosport Tube, was first used prior to WW I.

Before the Cadet climbed into the airplane, it was necessary for him to make a preflight inspection. This entailed walking around the airplane and looking for any unusual conditions, such as engine oil leaks, fabric condition, tire inflation, damage to landing gear struts, control surfaces, fuel supply and other similar details.

Preflight finished, it was now into the airplane: make sure that the parachute leg straps are now fastened; pull the seat belt tight; and listen while the Instructor goes through the start up check list.

It would be nice to say that the engine roared into life. However, that would be a gross overstatement. The five cylinder Kinner just did not have the capability to ROAR. The sound of the engine was best described by one of our ground school Instructors. When describing to the class how to remember the engine firing order, he said "The firing order of the Kinner engine is: ONE -THREE - FIVE - TWO - FOUR - PUTT - PUTT!!" He obviously made his point. After more than 50 years, I still remember.

As the engine came to life, the little airplane shook and shuttered and it quickly became apparent that the goggles were not just for the Aviator Look but were very much needed to keep the wind out of your eyes. The windscreen (not windshield) didn't offer much protection from the propeller blast.

The next step was to taxi the airplane out to the runway. The trip to the runway was a series of small turns, first to the left and then to the right, so that the track was like that of a snake. This was necessary since it was not possible to see straight ahead over the nose of the airplane. Before turning onto the runway, the plane was turned into the wind and stopped so that the engine could be run up to check magnetos, oil pressure, and power.

Now was the time to wait for the control tower to give us a green light, indicating clearance to move to the runway and take off. Soon, we were accelerating down the runway and shortly we lifted into the sky. My second flight. The first was as a passenger in a Ford Trimotor quite a few years earlier. On this takeoff I would again be a passenger. However, this would also be the last time for quite a while. Soon, I would be doing all the "work".

Once clear of the traffic pattern, the Instructor said: "Put your feet on the rudder pedals and grasp, LIGHTLY, the control stick. Now, follow through as I make a few maneuvers." Before long, he turned over the controls to me and I WAS FLYING!! However, although my intent was to fly straight and level, we did quite a lot of going up and going down and skidding and sliding around the sky.

After about three quarters of an hour, the first flight was over. While I had actually done little, I was tired, but I felt GREAT!!

In the next three weeks I accumulated a little over eleven and one quarter hours of instruction. These hours were filled with stalls (with power on and with power off), spins, landings, lazy eights, loops and the whole gamut of aerial maneuvers.

On July 15, 1943, the Instructor made "the" decision. It was now the time for me to try to do it all by myself!!

THAT WAS A REALLY GREAT FLIGHT. For almost half an hour I was up there all alone. While I had been forewarned that the airplane would perform much differently without the Instructor's weight, it now seemed as if I had a hold of a really hot airplane. That perception disappeared when it came time to land. Then it seemed as if the thing would never quit flying. It wanted to float forever. However, the plane did touch down on the runway on the first attempt with an adequate amount of "hard stuff" left in front of me. I had SOLOED. I was now a REAL aviator!

If a list of the instruments devised by man to torture man were made, the Link Instrument Trainer must certainly take its place on this list. Near the top.

The Link Trainer was among the first, if not THE first, flight simulator designed and put to use. Its purpose was to acquaint pilots with the instruments and techniques used for instrument or "blind" flying.

WALTER, J. C.
I'm WACY, but I'm going to Long Beach.

THE YOUNG AVIATOR
from the
EAGLES LOG
CLASS 44-A EDITION
DOS PALOS ARMY AIR BASE

When flying in dense fog or clouds, the pilot is unable to literally tell up from down. Without instruments to guide him the pilot is helpless. I realize that, unless one has experienced actually controlling an airplane in zero visibility conditions, it is difficult to understand the implications involved with "blind" flying.

To create the illusion that there was a connection between the Link Trainer and a real airplane, the trainer body, a chunky little fuselage, was fitted with rudimentary wings and a tail assembly. No propeller, engine or landing gear. Hinged on the left side of the fuselage was a box-like affair which swung up over the top of the fuselage and completely obscured the outside world from the eyes of the student. Oh yes, the little "airplane" was painted in Army Air Force blue and yellow, with insignia.

It was now our time to be introduced to this small tilting box on a swivel.

The student climbed into the bigger box, put on a headset (now his only link to the outside world) and closed the smaller box. The inside of the trainer was equipped with a control stick, rudder pedals and a throttle. A bunch of dials and instruments glowed eerily from the instrument panel.

As the torture session began, the Instructor requested the student to execute a series of maneuvers, using the instruments to direct and monitor what the little beast was doing. All too often, the session became a game of chasing the needles on the gauges.

A moving "bug" on the Instructor's table plotted the movement of the "airplane" on a paper chart. At times, the trace resembled the trail of a drunken cockroach.

Although the pace of the training was crowded, there was time to relax and become better acquainted with each other. This off-duty time combined with the relative smallness of our living quarters led to some good and close friendships. Among these were two friends, Bill Noland and Bob Perry, who were especially close.

On our first leave, Bill and I took off for San Francisco. We left Dos Palos Saturday noon after inspection and hitch hiked to the City-By-The-Bay. We had no trouble getting rides. Our first stop in San Francisco was the Top of the Mark. We had heard about this huge bar, dining room and ballroom located on the top of the Mark Hopkins Hotel and wanted to see it first hand. The place, surprisingly, was full of civilians with only a few military types scattered about. Fortunately for us, these civilians wanted to show their support of the War Effort by buying drinks for these brave young aviators. We, of course, did not want to disappoint or discourage them; so, we let them. It was a great weekend. In fact, some of that weekend's activities were the origin of the quote printed under my picture in the Eagle's Log, Class 44-A.

On Sunday we thumbed our way back to Dos Palos without a bit of trouble.

Being a hitch hiking Aviation Cadet did have its drawbacks. All too often, the driver upon finding out we were budding pilots, would proceed to demonstrate that he could make his automobile fly, well, almost fly. Some rides were real "white knucklers".

Most unfortunately, that trip turned out to be Bill's last weekend leave. On Thursday, July 30, a plane, flown by Bill and his Instructor, was involved in a mid air collision with another PT-22, a plane that also had a student and an Instructor aboard. Bill and both Instructors were killed. The other student managed to parachute to safety.

I was flying solo in the vicinity of the collision. Although I did not see the actual collision, I did see the two planes as they splashed into a rice paddy. The PT-22 was not equipped with a radio, so I immediately headed back to the Field, as fast as the plane would go, to report the accident. At the time, I did not know who was involved or the seriousness of the accident. I landed and taxied to the ramp,

BILL NOLAND

BOB PERRY

shut down the engine and yelled to a line girl that there had been a crash and gave her the location. I got out of the plane and went to the ready room to see if they had any information. They didn't. In a short time, my Instructor came out of the Instructor's Lounge and said that we were going up for some dual. Later, I suspected that he knew that Bill had been killed and knowing that Bill and I were good friends, decided that it would be a good idea to get me back in the air —- to forestall a possible case of "buck fever".

Obviously, this accident put a damper upon things for some time. It was the first accident resulting in fatalities in Eagle Field history. It really brought home the fact that although flying was fun, it could also be very deadly.

We were never officially told how the accident happened. Our speculation was that one of the planes had executed a stall and in the process of recovery it dived onto the top of Bill's plane. Why the Instructor in the plane doing stalls did not bail out was unclear. There was the possibility that he had been knocked unconscious in the accident and thus was unable to bail out before the plane hit the ground.

All through our training, it had been drilled into us: "Keep your head and eyes moving." "You never hit the airplane you see." "ALWAYS 'clear' the area before doing aerobatics." After this accident, all eyes were moving like flies in an empty pop bottle and all heads were swiveling to the extent that a smoking neck wouldn't have been much of a surprise.

Difficult as it was, I could not let myself become another victim of Bill's accident. Helping me to put things in perspective was the hectic pace of the training program.

Having over twenty hours flying time, I was beginning to feel really comfortable in the air. Before each solo flight the Instructor would give us assignments of maneuvers to practice. So, on these occasions it would be off into the "blue" and then head out to the

34

practice area which was some distance from the field. On the way to and from the practice area would be "my" time —- time to lazily wander through the sky, enjoy the sights and marvel at the fact that I was actually flying all by myself.

On really clear days it was possible to see the mountains off toward Yosemite to the east, a hint of the ocean over the top of the mountains to the west and the vast expanse of the San Joaquin Valley to the north and south. Also watch the trains, like well disciplined worms, glide along the silver threads of the rails. See ant-like people scurrying about in their activities and the bug-like automobiles crawling along their well laid out pathways.

It was almost unbelievable. In a few short months I had gone from being earth bound to having the whole sky to explore!

Upon reaching the halfway point in Primary Training, Cadets were allowed to have an automobile. Therefore, on the first weekend after reaching the midpoint, I decided to try to make it to Long Beach and bring back my car. The mission was successfully accomplished. Now, on weekends we could go to the L.A. area —- a 600 mile round trip which had to be accomplished between noon Saturday and 7:00 P.M. Sunday.

There were, however, a couple of catches. The first, and the most important, was gasoline. The "A" ration, the only one for which I qualified, wouldn't cover even one trip a month. However, Betsy would hold six trim Cadets with only a little squeezing. With five eager passengers, gasoline was never a problem. We used every class and denomination of gasoline ration coupon that existed. From "T" (Farm Tractor) to all of the passenger car and truck coupons. To service station operators, who were solely in the business of selling gasoline, a coupon was a coupon. No questions asked.

The second, and equally serious, catch was the tires on old Betsy. They had been regrooved (grooves cut into the remaining thin layer of rubber to create what looked like tread but actually did little to improve traction), but now again they were almost as smooth as a billiard ball. Recaps or replacements just were not to be had with my status and contacts. Later, this catch would prove to be the more serious.

Bob Perry was on board for every trip. He lived in Hawthorne, California. Before joining the Cadets he had been in the movie business. I'm not sure in what connection; however, he was acquainted with Andy Devine, among others. So, one Sunday, on our way back to Dos Palos, we stopped by Andy's place. Unfortunately, Andy was not at home; however, his wife was. Now, Andy may have had a gravel voice, been more than a little on the heavy side, always the sidekick and never the hero; HOWEVER, judging from his wife, he sure could pick 'em!!

On the last weekend trip to the L.A. area, luck ran out. We were somewhat late in getting started back. So, it was necessary to push Betsy for all she was worth. Coming down the Grapevine Grade and onto the long straight down grade into Bakersfield we were really rolling along. (Well over the 45 mph speed limit.) Then, it happened. The right front tire called it quits with a loud bang. I managed to keep the car on the road and get stopped. Fortunately, there was a spare; however, the reason that it was a spare was because it was the worst one of the lot. After changing tires, we were off again. Keeping in mind the fragility of the right front tire, I held our speed to a somewhat reduced level —— almost to the legal limit. The combination of a late start, the time it took to change the tire and the necessary reduction in speed combined to make it very obvious: "We aren't going to get back to the Base before the 7:00 P.M. deadline!!"

Such was indeed the case. We finally reached Dos Palos about 9:30 P.M. I pulled into the parking lot and drove along the unlighted portion of the fence. The passengers slipped out of the car into the dark and went in over the fence. Unfortunately, for me, the designated Cadet parking area was well lit and easily watched by the gate guard. There was no sneaking over the fence for me.

I was not surprised when on Monday morning I was summoned to Headquarters. It was a very short session. The judgment: 50 tours and confined to Base until I was transferred to my next station.

A "tour" was one hour of marching. At Santa Ana tour marching was done with a rifle. At Dos Palos the rifle was replaced with a strapped on parachute.

After undergoing this nonsense of marching with a parachute for about ten hours, I reasoned there should be some other way to get this penalty served to the satisfaction of the Military. And, coincidentally, to relieve me from the annoying butt bumping by the parachute pack.

Since I had to check in and out before and after each tour walked, I had become rather well acquainted with the Cadet Office Staff. One day, I asked if it would be possible for me to work off the remaining tours by applying my meager typing talents to some of their office work. A deal was struck. The fact that one of the office staff, a Sergeant, had attended Franklin College helped. Hoosier helping Hoosier. The rest of the tours were completed by sitting on my butt instead of having it pummeled by a parachute pack. There are times when everybody wins. This was one of them.

The end of the training period neared. Now, we were sent off on solo cross country trips. This involved mapping out our course, following it to another field, landing, taking off and finding the way back to Dos Palos. We were timed on take off, checked in and out at the intermediate field and checked in at Dos Palos. With these checks, the Instructors could be sure that we hadn't gotten lost or indulged in some buzzing or other prohibited side excursions.

When landing at the intermediate field we were told to make a short field landing. For this, the PT-22 was admirably equipped.

The landing flaps were actuated by a handle along the left side of the cockpit. Pumping the handle up and down through the upper one

37

half of its travel caused the flaps to be lowered about five degrees with each stroke. Pushing the handle all of the way down caused the flaps to rapidly retract to the full up position.

So, when making a short field landing, we would pump on full flaps and drag the airplane down the final at just over stalling speed. As soon as the fence was cleared and we were over the runway, we would push the flap control handle all the way down causing the flaps to completely retract, the airplane to drop to the runway like a rock and stick there as if it were glued. The observing Instructor was too far away to see what had gone on with the flaps, we thought. It's possible he knew but just decided not to make an issue of it.

While this system of flap control had its advantage for short field landings, it could cause trouble at other times — for instance, when a pilot was making a landing with partial flaps and it became necessary to apply more flaps. Panic pumping with the inadvertent pushing of the handle all the way down would result in the flaps being retracted completely. This was guaranteed to screw up even the best planned approach and landing. Do this a time or two and you had better become more careful pretty quickly. The Instructor took a very dim view of a missed approach and the following go-around.

Now it was time for the final check ride. This one would be with a Second Lieutenant. Previous check rides had been with a civilian Instructor, other than our regular one. I was pretty comfortable about the ground school grades. Moreover, the fifty tours had been completed so that slate was clean. If I could pass this check ride, I would be on my way to Basic Flight School.

The ride was uneventful. No big mistakes. The FIRST BIG HURDLE WAS PASSED!!! I HAD MADE IT THROUGH PRIMARY!!!

On August 24, 1943, I took my last ride in the PT-22. I now had the grand total of more than 65 hours flying time. Of this, almost 35 hours were solo.

It now looked like the chances were pretty good that the next move would be on to Basic Flight School. The question was: Where?

Then, the word was passed. Final ratings and next assignments were posted on the bulletin board. A mad scramble ensued. A mob of Cadets surrounded the bulletin board. Each Cadet searched the various lists as he looked for his name. There were yells of joy and moans of agony. Moans of agony resulting from the knowledge that their Pilot Training was ending.

I was one of those yelling for joy. First, because I had passed and, second, I was headed for Basic Flight School in Lancaster, California, about 75 miles from Long Beach.

The Saturday night before graduation Sunday we had a dance. The band was Xavier Cugat with the Camel Caravan. Billie came up from Long Beach for the dance. When class 43-L graduated, Ted Lewis' band had been the featured entertainment. Captain Smith, the Commanding Officer, obviously had a direct connection with Hollywood.

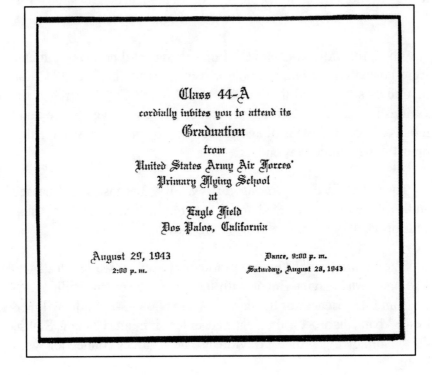

Class 44-A
cordially invites you to attend its
Graduation
from
United States Army Air Forces'
Primary Flying School
at
Eagle Field
Dos Palos, California

August 29, 1943
2:00 p. m.

Dance, 9:00 p. m.
Saturday, August 28, 1943

CHAPTER 5
BASIC FLIGHT SCHOOL

I was given permission to make the transfer from Dos Palos to Lancaster in Betsy. However, Captain Smith would not give permission for me to take any passengers. The trip was uneventful and made well within the speed limit only for this simple reason: Don't overstress Betsy's thin soled "shoes".

My luck still held. Not only did Betsy's shoes make the trip but Lancaster turned out to also be a Civilian operated school. In fact, it was the only U.S.A.A.F. Basic Flight School not operated by the Military. Before being used as a U.S.A.A.F. Training Base, RAF pilots had been trained there. It was older than Dos Palos, thus it was not quite as plush as Dos Palos. However, it had to be far more relaxed and comfortable than a similar Military operated base. Before being converted to an Army Basic Flight School and renamed War Eagle Field, it was known as Polaris Flight Academy. The owner and operator was a Major Moseley. He also owned and operated a number of Army Primary Flight Schools through out California.

It was now time to become acquainted with the Vultee BT-13. Compared to the PT-22, this airplane was a giant. No more puny five cylinder engine. Here was a big nine cylinder radial that looked and sounded like a big round airplane engine should.

The official name of the BT-13 was the Valiant; however, it was more commonly, although not with affection, called the Vibrator. This latter name was bestowed for two reasons. First, in flight, the cockpit canopy rattled almost constantly. Second, when operated at full throttle, with the prop set in low pitch and all 450 horses pulling, the noise level it created seemed capable of vibrating the whole universe.

In most large radial engines, there is a set of reduction gears between the engine crankshaft and the propeller. This results in the propeller rotating at a slower speed than does the engine crankshaft. However, the BT engine did not have reduction gears. Thus, the propeller turned at the same speed as the engine crankshaft. In low pitch the speed of the big prop was fast enough for the tips to exceed the speed of sound. This was the cause of the unholy racket emitted during take off and initial climb out.

The BT also brought some new elements of flight: two (high and low) propeller pitch settings, a full instrument panel (for night and "blind" flying), a two way radio which could also be used for communication between the front and rear seats, trim tabs for all control surfaces, sliding cockpit canopy and solo from the front seat.

The two pitch propeller settings were comparable to a two speed transmission in an automobile. Low pitch was used for take off and climbing and high pitch was used for cruising and high speed let down.

My Instructor was Otho O. "Red" Donaghue. Given his name, it is probably redundant to say that he was a big, red haired Irishman.

On September 7, 1943, after successfully passing the blindfold cockpit check, Red and I went off in the BT. The purpose of the blindfold cockpit check was to make sure that the Pilot knew, without having to look, the location of every control, switch and instrument. This knowledge greatly reduced the Pilot's reaction time both in normal aircraft operation and, more importantly, in the case of emergency situations.

Since we were supposed to now know how to fly, there was none of that "Follow through with the Instructor" stuff. On take off, HE followed YOU through. Take off was a new experience. When that BIG engine was a given full throttle and took hold of things, the airplane developed a mind of its own. And, it definitely did not want to go straight down the runway. I soon became aware that it was going to take an awful lot of rudder to keep this beast going where I was supposed to take it.

While the struggle between man (me) and beast (the BT) was going on, Red rather sarcastically asked over the intercom: "Why don't you use the damn rudder trim tab. That's what the thing's for." After that, take offs were not too bad. The PT-22 didn't have a rudder trim tab for the simple reason that it didn't need one. The BT definitely needed one and you better use it.

The daily schedule was a busy one.
Typically:
  5:45 A.M. Reville
  6:00 A.M. Breakfast
  7:00 A.M. to 12:00 P.M. Flightline
  12:15 P.M. Lunch
  1:00 P.M. to 4:00 P.M. Ground School
  4:15 P.M. to 4:45 Drill
  4:50 P.M. to 5:45 Calisthenics
  6:00 P.M. Supper
  7:00 P.M. to 7:15 P.M. Retreat
  7:30 P.M. to 9:30 P.M. Ground School
           Link Trainer or Study Time
  9:45 P.M. Lights Out

After about five and three-quarters hours of dual, I was turned loose on my own. It was Wednesday, September 15, 1943.

Things had begun to speed up. There was instrument time (under a very hot, black, blind flying hood), formation flying, navigation (cross country), night flying and, of course, more Link Trainer.

For night flying, the aircraft was equipped with non-flashing red (left) and green (right) navigation lights on the wing tips and a white light on the tail. The predecessor to today's rotating beacon and strobe light was a steady red light called a passing light. It was mounted in the leading edge of the left wing, along side of the left landing light. This light could only be seen from directly ahead. The steadily burning navigation lights made it easy to confuse the lights of an airplane with a star and vice versa. As a result, some wild night aerobatics were executed as the Pilot tried to avoid a head on collision with Mars or some other distant heavenly body.

On the first night flight I almost jumped out of the airplane as it started down the runway on take off. When the throttle was opened and as the engine accelerated, a tremendous flame came out of the engine exhaust stack extending along the right side of the fuselage almost to the rear seat. I thought, for sure, that the airplane was on fire. Turned out that the flame was always there. In daylight it just couldn't be seen. Once the airplane was off of the ground and in the air and the power cut back and the fuel-air ratio reduced, the flame retreated back into the exhaust pipe. At night, this flame made it especially easy to adjust the engine fuel mixture. Richen the mixture and the flame got longer and redder. Lean the mixture and the flame got shorter and turned from orange-white to blue.

One of the points in night flying that Red stressed was that we be able to land without the use of the landing lights. His reasoning was that under certain combat security conditions you could not use landing lights.

Further, there was always the possibility that the lights might not work. After a while, we found that it was as easy to land without lights as it was with them.

My first night solo flight had its own very special surprise. Lancaster was far enough inland to be exempt from the costal brown/black out. On my first night solo I was up tooling about the sky admiring the lights below and keeping my eyes on the move for the sight of another airplane. There was very little night traffic and, as a result, I was really enjoying the scenery below.

Then, suddenly, all of the lights on the ground disappeared. My first reaction: "My God, there's an air raid and they've turned off all of the lights. This means that the field is shut down, too." Then came such thoughts as: I could get shot down. Or, I might have to stay up here until I run out of fuel and have to jump in the dark. A really distressing thought. Confirming my assessment of the situation that things were in dire straits was the ominous silence of the control tower radio.

As I tried to figure a way out of my dilemma, I looked out at the wing lights and saw a halo round them. Then it dawned upon me (much to my relief), I had flown into a cloud. There was no blackout nor was there any air raid. As soon as I flew out of the cloud, the lights on the ground reappeared.

The fact that Lancaster was in the Mojave Desert and close to a number of large dry lakes gave us an advantage that no other Basic Flying School had —- that was the chance to make a real instrument landing. With the Instructor in the back of the airplane (a must when the student was flying under the hood), the student would line the plane up with one of the lakes. He then would set up his approach let down, hold everything steady and fly the airplane onto the ground. The dry lakes were miles in diameter and as smooth as a table top. There was little chance of either under or overshooting the landing.

In the group of students assigned to "Red" was a fellow from Montana, Habert E. Underwood, better known as "Undie". One day Undie and Red were up doing aerobatics which, by itself, was not particularly out of the ordinary. What happened, was.

The seats in the BT had a height adjusting mechanism utilizing a type of ratchet system with a locking lever.

One of the aerobatic maneuvers Red and Undie were doing was a loop. As Undie came out of the bottom of one of these he really pulled her back hard. Apparently the height adjustment of Red's seat was not securely locked. The G's of Undie's recovery were enough to cause the lock to disengage. Red's seat let go and hit the bottom of its travel with a bang. The combination of the G's created by the maneuver and those resulting when the seat hit its stop turned Red's lights out. Out, completely. Undie heard and felt Red and the seat hit the bottom of the seat's travel. His first concern was that he had broken something. Looking around to see what had happened, Undie saw Red slumped over and out like a light.

After a little while, Red came to, eyes watering and obviously wondering what had happened. After that episode, every time one of us students pulled a few G's with Red along, we'd ask him if he had blacked out. This freedom to banter with the Instructor was one of the big pluses of attending a Civilian run school.

It was now the practice to allow two students to go up in the same airplane. This obviously provided an opportunity for one student to impress the other with his superior flying skills.

One of the stories associated with this practice was told as a true story. I don't know whether or not it really happened, but that is incidental.

The radio in the BT served both as radio and an intercom between the front and rear seats. A switch to select either "radio" or "intercom" was mounted on the right side of the forward and aft cockpits. In this story, two students were flying together and obviously one was trying aerobatics. The radio selector switch, instead of being set to "intercom", was set to "radio". The student doing the flying had just completed a maneuver. Thinking he was on intercom, he commented the other student: "I sure f——d that one up!!"

46

Immediately, the tower operator came back with: "The aircraft that just made that transmission, identify yourself."

The student's reply was: "I'm not that f——d up!!"

One day, having nothing better to do I decided to find out how high the old BT-13 could go. After 45 minutes and 40 gallons of fuel, I managed to get her up to 17,500 feet. The airplane was still climbing at 250 feet/minute. However, having on just a light gabardine flight suit and no gloves, the 23° F temperature forced me to abort my climb and return to the warmer earth.

Being as close as we were to Burbank, where P-38's were built, we frequently had P-38's visiting the field. Pilots on test flights would drop in to visit. One of the Pilots who visited us often was Tony Lavier, Lockheed's Chief Test Pilot.

One afternoon, three Navy F-4U Corsairs on a ferry flight were diverted to Lancaster due to weather problems at their destination. The following morning, Tony arrived at the field just as the Navy Pilots were getting ready to leave. They had just preflighted their planes and were about to get in them to leave. Obviously proud of the Corsair, they challenged Tony to a mock dogfight. However, Tony declined.

They tried to persuade him, but he was adamant. Finally, they gave up and took off. However, before leaving the area they decided to "beat up" the field. That did it. Tony ran out and got into the '38. He cranked up the starboard engine and began rolling to the active runway. On the way he started the port engine. No engine warm up nor preflight run up. Off he went. Tony knew the strengths of the '38 and proceeded to use them. These strengths consisted of the ability to out-climb and out-dive practically any other aircraft flying. The Corsairs never could get near him. Soon they disappeared to the North. Tony came over the field, gave a victory roll and went back to Burbank.

At the mid point of the stay at Basic the time came to make a decision. Did I want to go to single engine or multi-engine advanced flight school? Of course, this choice could be academic if I failed to pass my final check ride and the ground school courses. Another, and equally important factor in this decision, was: which kind of Pilot did the U.S.A.A.F. need the most?

My choice was the result of taking into account both desire and practicality. Probably, to a man, the overwhelming desire of every Cadet was to be a single engine fighter Pilot. However, the reality of the situation indicated that the U.S.A.A.F. probably needed at least twice as many multi-engine Pilots. So, if you went to single engine advanced and were not among the very, very top, the chance was extremely high that you would wind up in the right hand (co-pilot) seat of a multi-engine airplane. My position was: if I was going to be in a multi-engine aircraft, I wanted the left hand (pilot) seat. So, following through, I applied for twin-engine advanced.

On October 27, 1943 I took my last flight, for a while, in the BT.

I now had 141:52 total flying hours of which 67:22 were solo.

As at Dos Palos, the postings of the passing/failing list and the next station assignment lists were anxiously awaited. Finally, they were posted.

I Passed!! Next assignment: Twin Engine Advanced Flight Training, Douglas, Arizona.

I was still in Pilot training. Only one more step to go to get those silver Wings!!

For Primary and Basic I had been fortunate to have been able to stay in California, thus, reasonably close to Long Beach and all of its interests. However, this string of luck had just come to its end.

Douglas was close to only the barren wastes of southern Arizona and northern Mexico.

Even if Betsy's tired old shoes could have made it to Douglas, the Base C.O. said: "No." So, the time came to part with her. The next week end I took her back to Long Beach and left her there, and hitch hiked back to Lancaster.

CHAPTER 6
ADVANCED FLIGHT SCHOOL

My one and only previous troop train experience had involved the use of some unrestored day coaches which must have been plucked from some museum storage shed. This time we were treated better. We had Pullmans!! I don't recall how long it took us to make the trip from Lancaster to Douglas, but it seemed as if we went into a siding even for slow freight trains going in the same direction.

It was the first of November when we finally pulled into the Douglas train station. Still in our summer uniforms we stepped off of the train into what seemed like a refrigerator. Given the time of year, Douglas' altitude of over 4,000 feet and an ever-blowing wind, it was nothing but cold. Having enjoyed California's "year round summer" for the preceding three plus years, this came as a definite shock to my system.

We were in the Army. There was no mistake about it! This was an Army run school. No more cozy quarters. There were now single story temporary Army barracks. In a letter home I described them as "A sprinkling of 2 x 4's held together by Celotex." The "facility" was in a separate building about 1/2 block away. The last Army barracks I had graced with my presence were at Santa Ana. Those were two story and substantially constructed. Plus, the "facility" was built in.

Other features of the Army such as Mess Management and Guard duty as well as all of the trappings of Army life reappeared.

Realizing that there was nothing we could do about our accommodations, we settled in and began to eagerly look forward to becoming acquainted with our next aircraft to master. This turned out to be the Cessna AT-17 Bobcat; also known as the Bamboo Bomber or the Polecat or Bamboo Beaufighter. The first nickname stemmed from the fact that the airplane was made mostly of wood and fabric. I don't believe that I ever flew an AT-17 that did not have the presence of a cracked main wing spar written up on the Form 5. However, I don't recall ever having heard of this crack causing a wing to break off.

On November 11, I took my first flight. After 4 hours of dual it was off on my own with another Student Pilot. The AT-17 was an easy and enjoyable airplane to fly. It was about the same size as the BT-13; although the AT-17 was a bit heavier, the two 245 HP Jacobs engines made it a bit faster than the single 450 HP Pratt & Whitney engine could move the BT.

It was now time to learn the idiosyncrasies of a twin engine aircraft and deal with the presence of a retractable landing gear. It turned out that the retractable landing gear was also something to have fun with.

In ground school they told us about how it had been made impossible to retract the landing gear while the plane was sitting on the ground. This safety feature was accomplished by putting electrical switches on the main landing gear struts. When the airplane's weight compressed the shocks, the switches opened the retracting mechanism circuit, thus making it impossible to raise the landing gear.

This system design unintentionally, I'm sure, provided a means to show off in what was really a rather drab airplane.

The "stunt": Near the end of the takeoff roll the Pilot holds slight forward control column pressure to keep the weight on the mains and the shocks compressed; then the Pilot or Copilot flips the gear switch to the "Retract" position. When more than enough flying speed is reached, the Pilot hauls "the bird" off of the runway. The landing gear immediately starts to retract. From the ramp this looks like a Pilot that's really on top of his airplane.

As with most tricks, there are things that can go wrong —- such as pulling the plane off the runway before adequate airspeed is reached. Do this and the ship rises just enough to unload the shocks and start the gear coming up. But there is not enough speed to fly. The plane sinks back toward the runway and the taxpayers have just bought at least a couple of propellers. Usually considerably more.

This happened once while I was at Douglas. No, it was not I.

Also as a part of the landing gear retracting system is a warning horn mounted in the cockpit. If the throttles are closed with the landing gear retracted, the horn blasts in the Pilot's ear. This warning device gave rise to an interesting story.

The Pilot had turned on final approach with the landing gear still retracted. The control tower operator noticed this and radioed the Pilot. "Aircraft on final approach, your landing gear is retracted!! Acknowledge!!" This was repeated several times with no reply. Finally, the Pilot came on with: "Tower, repeat your message. Can't hear a thing with this damned horn blowing in my ear."

It did not take long for us to have it confirmed that we were back in the Army. We had a Tactical Officer (Ground Pounder) by the name of Lt. Rosen. He was something. (When you accidentally stick your finger with a needle, there is a verb that adequately describes what happened. This same word, as slang, may also be used as a noun to describe a part of the male anatomy. This noun fitted the Lieutenant perfectly.)

Douglas, a town of less than 9,000 people, was overwhelmed by the presence of the Air Field. Off the Base, there was absolutely nothing to do and no place to do it. The few girls in the town were outnumbered by the scores of Cadets and Base Personnel.

When I took Betsy back to Long Beach before leaving Lancaster for Douglas, Billie and I, by mutual agreement, had called it quits. Without that attachment, I was now back in circulation. One big problem, there was no one with which to circulate in Douglas.

However, Undie and I did manage to have a little success in finding companionship. I became acquainted with a telephone operator and he with her mother. However, my Army arranged schedule and her Telephone Company arranged schedule were seldom in sync. It never turned out to be a really successful arrangement for me. According to Undie, he had somewhat better luck, I believe.

When allowed in town on the weekends, we had to be off the streets by 11:00 P.M. One Saturday night Undie and I missed the last bus for the Base and were without a place to stay. We thought we could solve the problem by holing up in the USO which was located in the Gadsden Hotel. The Gadsden was the center of the town. In fact, it was the center of the adjacent Universe. We started the night's sleep by curling up on the sofas. However, as the night wore on, it became cold, and we were without any covers. First, we thought about using the drapes, but we couldn't figure out how to get them down without inflicting serious damage to them. The problem was solved by our lying on floor and folding a rug over us. The one fault with this solution however was when the rug was turned upside down, all the sand and dirt in it fell out on top of us. When dawn broke, we gratefully headed back to the Base to get warm and clean. As a result of this more than miserable night, never again did we get trapped in town without a place to stay.

On Christmas Eve several of us decided to go to Tucson. However, the "rewards" of being there were just not worth the length (about 3 hrs. each way) and the cost ($3.10) of the bus trip there and back.

We did have a good time, engaging in such fun as "Drinking Beer in the Pioneer (Hotel).", but we never felt the urge to repeat the visit.

We were now no longer living in two man rooms but open barracks. This presented both a large arena and an audience for practical jokes. The antics and reactions of the "trickee" could be seen and appreciated by a goodly number of people.

"Hot foots" were common. A "Hot Foot" is created by placing the head of one or more paper matches in the space where the shoe upper meets the shoe sole. The victim would be distracted by a Cadet while another Cadet placed the matches and lit the match paper sticks. The paper would burn down until the heads of the matches were ignited. The heat thus generated would be intense; however, by the time the victim felt the initial warmth and before he could untie his shoe and get it off, the heat really built to a painful level. Earlier in our Army career we had found that a small dab of shoe polish placed on the head of the match/es would substantially increase both the length and the temperature of the "burn". Some "jokers" would crawl under the beds on their stomachs the length of the barracks to "nail" the unsuspecting one.

Short sheeting was another favorite trick. This operation was reserved particularly for those who habitually returned to the barracks right at lights out time or a little past. The confusion as the "trickee" tried to figure things out in the dark was most rewarding. Especially, if the victim had been drinking. As was usually the case.

Another trick was to fill a rubber (condom) with water, tie the open end closed and lay it in the middle of the bed between the sheets. The unsuspecting one would dive into the bed and burst the rubber and wind up soaking wet and with a bed full of water.

On one occasion this particular trick almost had serious consequences. We had set up Undie's bed. After a visit with the telephone operator's mother, he came in just after lights out, carrying a pretty good load. Without benefit of underwear or pajamas, which was his habit, Undie slid into bed and immediately burst the rubber. Naked, angry and staggering he lurched from the bed and began shaking the water off while expressing his opinion of anybody who would pull this sort of trick. In the bed next to Undie was Ernest Tubbs. Tubbs was unaware of the trick and was sound asleep. That is, until Undie started raising a huge commotion. Tubbs felt the water splashing on his face which awakened him. Then, in the dim light he saw Undie's "equipment" flying around just above his face. Although Tubbs' conclusion was incorrect, it was possible to understand how he had reached it. Cooler heads intervened to prevent a fight.

During the war there was a scarcity of whisky. However, just across the border from Douglas was a small Mexican town, Agua Prieta, consisting of a few adobe buildings. Completing the picture of a "typical" Mexican village, as often seen in the movies of the day, were lots of kids, dirt streets and sombrero wearing males. In that little village lay the solution to our whiskey shortage. They had <u>Juarez American Whiskey</u> available at something less than an exorbitant price. This attraction, alone, caused us to occasionally cross the border.

Agua Prieta, in spite of its small size, had a very extensive Red Light District. Given the dearth of female companionship in Douglas, it would be expected that this "facility" would get considerable play by the Cadets. This was not the case. The real reason was the fact that soldiers from nearby Fort Huachuca were usually lined up in front of the brothel doors.

While at Douglas I experienced one of the most spectacular in-flight sights I've ever seen. It was a night flight with a full winter's moon. The air was perfectly clear. Scattered across the sky were a few very large, puffy and very white fair weather cumulus clouds. "Framing" the scene were ridges of snow capped mountains.

I don't recall what we were supposed to have been doing that night. Whatever it was, we didn't get it done. We spent our time touring around the sky and the clouds admiring and drinking in the spectacle.

In the last half of our stay at Douglas we were sent to an auxiliary field at Hereford, Arizona for a week. The purpose of this excursion was to simulate a primitive combat airfield situation. They did a damn good job simulating. The barracks were minimally equipped and cold. The food was barely edible. When the tour was over, we were glad to go back to Douglas, believe it or not.

In order to both fully utilize the aircraft and the Base facilities, we were often assigned to unusual scheduling. This is an example:

Flying - 11:30 P.M. to 6:00 A.M.;
Breakfast - 6:00 A.M.
Sleeping - 7:00 A.M.
Lunch - 2:00 P.M.
Ground School - 3:00 P.M.
Calisthenics - 5:00 P.M.
Drill - 6:30 P.M.
Dinner - 8:00 P.M.
Link Trainer - 9:00 P.M.

It was when I was on one of these schedules that I wrote the folks: "From the way things appear one has to be an idiot to get into this Air Corps and a superman to stay in."

At that time, the transcontinental airways were marked for night flying by rotating beacons which were spaced about 10 miles apart. Flying an airway at night you would see ahead of you this line of beacons, like so many long white fingers beckoning you to come their way. Beacons located at places without adjacent landing facilities had a red light that flashed alternately with the white beacon. For those locations where there were lighted landing fields, a green light replaced the red light.

For a night auxiliary field we used the airways emergency field located at Cochise, Arizona. The field was unpaved and there were just enough runway lights to show where the edge of the graded surface of the runway was. One night, my fellow student and I, along with several other planes, were instructed to proceed to Cochise to shoot landings. Each student was to shoot two landings. As the parade of planes continued, the amount of dust being kicked up kept increasing. There was only a light wind, so the dust just hung over the field.

When the turn came for my partner's last landing, his approach was perfect, and, as he flared it out, the landing lights made it appear that we were at just the right height above the "runway". To both of us, this was going to be a real "grease job". However, there was no thump of the wheels hitting the ground. Suddenly, the airplane stopped flying and dropped about five feet to the runway. We hit so hard that all of the lights in the airplane blinked off and back on. My fellow student had made a perfect landing on the top of the dust cloud. (This could be one of the ways that the main wing spars got cracked.) We stopped, got out and looked over the landing gear but no evidence of damage was apparent. We flew back to Douglas and made a note in the Form 5 that the airplane had been landed rather hard.

Near the end of training, we had completed all of the required flying programs. We were sent out, two students to a plane, to build flying time and practice various maneuvers. On one of these flights Undie and I teamed up. We went out to the southeastern portion of the flying area, took off our headsets, pushed back the seats and put our feet on top of the rudder pedal support. In that comfortable and relaxed condition, we wandered aimlessly about the sky and engaged in a bull session. After some little time, one of us happened to look out the left side of the airplane. There was another AT-17 in close formation with us. The guy in the right hand seat was making all kinds of gestures toward his headset. It turned out to be a couple of Instructors who were checking to see whether or not the students were up there screwing off. We were caught red handed. On our way back we cooked up a story about how we had taken off our headsets so that we could better discuss the proper way to handle an engine failure on take off. They bought our story. Whew!!!

While at Douglas we learned how to fly in mountainous terrain. In addition to the well known up and down drafts encountered near mountains there is the less widely recognized box canyon danger.

This problem occurs when an airplane is flown at low altitude into the downhill end of a canyon. As flight up the canyon continues, the Pilot puts the airplane into a climb to keep his distance above the floor of the canyon. What he may fail to notice is that the canyon walls are rising faster than he is and that they are soon higher than the plane is. Also, the canyon walls are becoming closer together. Suddenly, the Pilot recognizes that he has a BIG problem. He is now in a situation where he has neither room between the canyon walls to make a 180° turn nor enough power and distance to climb over the canyon walls or the mountain in front of him. The resulting impact is almost always "deadening".

Near the end of December, 1943, we lost three airplanes on night flights. One of them was found immediately; the other two were not. In the sparsely settled area around us, both in Arizona and northern Mexico, a crash was not likely to be either observed or reported from the ground — particularly if it occurred at night and in the winter. I did not know any of the fellows involved.

Nearly 40 years later, in 1982, I visited the Pima Air Museum which is just outside of Tucson. Standing in the corner of the museum gift shop was a bent up prop. The tag on it stated it was from a wreck that was found in 1979. Through the serial number on the propeller the identification of the airplane had been traced. It was from one of the two planes from Douglas which had crashed in December 1943. The price for the relic was $45.00. Almost bought it. But then, what would I do with a bent up AT-17 prop? Nevertheless, the encounter "evaporated", for a short time, the present and whisked me back briefly into the past.

One of our last escapades at Douglas nearly got the whole class of 44-A thrown out of the place and into the walking Army. A new Cadet Lounge had just been completed. Naturally, such a worthy facility needed to be dedicated. So, a party was organized. The beer was cheap and plentiful, and there were plenty of participants.

In order to cool the beer it had been placed in a tank of ice and water. After a short time, immersion of the bottles in the water made the glue on the labels soft. With the glue soft, it was easy to slide the label off of the bottle. Once the label was in hand, a logical question was: "What to do with it?" One "genius" in the group figured out that if the label, glue side up, was placed on the side of his wallet, he could toss the wallet up to the twelve feet high ceiling. If the wallet hit the ceiling flat, the label would stick to the ceiling and his wallet would return to his hands. In less time that it takes to tell, the air was full of wallets and the ceiling was well decorated with beer bottle labels. As could have been predicted, Lt. Rosen disapproved of this conduct most strongly and was extremely upset with the results. Unfortunately, for the Lieutenant, our schedules and the time remaining did not provide an opportunity for a Class 44-A work detail to rectify the damage done. I suspect that chore was "enjoyed" by Class 44-B, our under class.

Unlike the procedure in Primary and Basic, where Cadets had to wait anxiously for the posting of results, those who had successfully made the grade were told somewhat in advance of the end of school. This was necessary in order for us to have time to buy and have fitted our officer's uniforms. This was one of the few times that the Military showed any real concern for the psyche of its people. We were given a $250.00 allowance for the purchase of new uniforms and I spent all but $20.00 of it. The winter blouse and pants came to $70.00; the gabardine trench coat, $60.00; shirts, $14.00 each and extra pants, $21.00/pair. We got to keep the Cadet issued underwear (olive drab!), socks and shoes.

By this time in the War, considerable concern had arisen within the non-flying Army that the Air Force branch was filling up with too many commissioned officers. A way to correct this problem was to appoint some of the flying school graduates as Flight (Warrant) Officers instead of Second Lieutenants. The uniforms of Flight

Officers and Commissioned Officers were the same, except for service cap and rank insignia. This then allowed the powers-that-were to hold to the last possible moment the announcement as to who received what rank which, in turn, gave the "wheels" the opportunity to add back some of the suspense of pass/fail that had been present at the previous two flight schools.

Finally, the announcement was made regarding who were to be 2nd Lieutenants and who were to be Flight Officers, and also, what and where our next assignment was. I lucked out again. I made 2nd Lieutenant and was assigned to B-17 Transition School at Hobbs, New Mexico. This was what I wanted, four engine transition school. Most of those who requested P-38's, B-25's etc. wound up either being sent to gunnery school to fly students or tow targets or to a Replacement Depot. There they would be assigned to the right seat of B-17's, B-24's, C-47's or other multi-engine airplanes.

It was time to turn in the Cadet uniform and serial number (19130275), put on the new officer's uniform and start remembering a new serial number (0-764529). Date of rank would be January 7, 1944. In just a little under 11 months I had learned to fly, had accumulated almost 269 hours flying time and received the rank of 2nd Lieutenant.

Now, came the time for us to be paid and given orders for our next assignment. In operations of this nature the procedure had always been to call out names one-by-one in alphabetical order starting with the letter "A". However, this time we would be called in reverse alphabetical order. Naturally, the change resulted in two choruses: one of joy and one of sorrow. For me, my name being near the end of the alphabet, meant that I got off the Base and into town among the first. Consequently, I was able to buy a ticket, get on the train and head for home soon after graduation. The last ones to get processed didn't' make it in time to catch the train and, as a result, had to spend a day of their leave in Douglas.

I was given a 10 day delay en route for the journey from Douglas to Hobbs. A long time before, I had decided to go home.

The Douglas Army Air Force
Pilot School

announces

the graduation of

Class 44-A

on Friday, January seventh

Nineteen hundred and forty-four

Douglas, Arizona

John C. Walter

LIEUTENANT, AIR CORPS
ARMY OF THE UNITED STATES

Now that I was officer, no longer did I travel with a barracks bag. The B-4 bag and the parachute bag took its place. The B-4 bag was a great piece of luggage. It will hold more stuff than you can carry.

By the same token, so will the parachute bag, being nothing more than a grossly oversized gym bag. For some reason or other, the people at Douglas thought it to be their duty to issue us a parachute, sheep skin lined winter flying jacket and pants, flying helmet and goggles. They knew where we were being assigned, and that probably when we reached the next base, we would immediately turn this gear in never to see it again. Either that thought never crossed their minds or they didn't care. We were destined to drag the stuff from Douglas to home and from home to Hobbs.

The trains were unbelievably crowded. In these circumstances, a huge heavy bag of unnecessary stuff was as unwelcome as a wheelbarrow full of bricks would have been. Once home, however, I did stage a fashion show by displaying the stuff to the folks as the pictures attest. Maybe this was why we were given it —- to show our folks that Uncle Sam was taking good care of their offspring. However, including the parachute also conveyed the wrong message, that is: "There's a chance something can go wrong."

While waiting in line at the Douglas railroad station to buy my ticket, I heard a soldier behind me say: "Lieutenant, sir, do you know how long it takes to get to Kansas City?" The question was asked several times. I began to wonder why the Lieutenant didn't answer the soldier. Suddenly, it dawned; I was the Lieutenant he was addressing. I just hadn't gotten used to being a Lieutenant.

The route involved the Southern Pacific from Douglas to El Paso; change at El Paso to another Southern Pacific train to Tucumcari, New Mexico; there change to the Rock Island (a real refugee operation) to Kansas City; in K.C. change to the Wabash for St. Louis; at St. Louis change to the Baltimore & Ohio for home. This all added up to two and one half days without a bath or a shower and without any opportunity of ever lying down. Meals were "catch as

| THE AUTHOR AND HIS MOTHER | THE "WELL DRESSED" AVIATOR |

you can". On the Rock Island segment I sat on the parachute bag in the aisle for the whole trip. (This use for the parachute bag almost, but not quite, compensated for the inconvenience of its presence.) As the then popular saying went: "Things are tough all over!". On this train ride they sure were.

CHAPTER 7
HOME LEAVE AND B-17 TRANSITION

I had not been home since Lee Craig and I were there in the summer of '42, which had been a year and half ago. There was a lot of time spent bringing the folks up to date on how great it was to fly, the tedium and silliness of some of the Army folderol and about all of the new territory I had seen. In the telling of the aerial exploits, it was very necessary to describe my close scrapes with disaster which had been averted only by the flying skills of their son. Mary Jane, my younger sister, being at the impressionable age of 16, was suitably awed by her brother's feats of daring-do with the silver wings being the icing on the cake.

Of course, as the taxpayers were paying for my fun, I had to let the local rate payers see what they were getting for their money. So, I managed to spread my presence around the town. Some of them were awed.

The ultimate showcase was the Friday night Washington High School basket-ball game. Servicemen were admitted without charge. With that added incentive, I went to the game. As I moved around the gym during half time, I encountered my former High School typing teacher selling soft drinks at the school's concession stand.

When I had been in her class, she had seemed much, much older than we students were. Then, she must have been all of 22. Now, some 5 years later, she didn't seem to be more than a few months older than I. Also, she was still unmarried. Though she wore glasses, she was still very attractive, an observation which had been made years ago.

During our conversation (not about typing) I suggested, perhaps, after the game we could go to Vincennes to see what was happening there. Vincennes was the ultimate "hot spot" for Washington. She thought that was a good idea. In fact, it was such a good idea, she managed to slip away from her game assignment before the game was over. As the outcome of the game could be learned from Saturday's paper, I could see no reason for me to hang around. We left for Vincennes.

We returned to her place around midnight. She asked me in. After we had been together for a while, there was a pounding at the door and a man's voice calling her name. She said it sounded like her boy friend, but not to pay any attention to him. He banged and yelled around for some time but then seemed to give up and leave. Since there were no lights on in the house, I don't know how he knew she was there. Maybe it was the strange car parked nearby. After some time, I left and went home. I didn't see him. However, he must have stayed out of sight somewhere nearby since later I learned he did see me leave.

Nevertheless they were ultimately married, so our one night fling must have caused no permanent damage to the relationship.

As it turned out, there was to be one more chapter to this episode.

When I got ready to leave Washington to go to Hobbs, Dad took me to the train station. While we were standing on the platform waiting for the train, who should walk by but the teacher's boy friend. Dad knew him, thus, an introduction was necessary.

No question, that was one time, for sure, when the phrase, "Glad to meet you," was not very sincere on the part of either party. I imagine the boy friend was glad to see me leaving town. Dad never knew that we, for a very short time, had at least one thing in common. Also, while we had not formally met before, we were not really total strangers.

B-17 TRANSITION

I was now off to my first posting as an officer. I was due to be in Hobbs by Tuesday midnight, January 18th, so I left Washington Sunday morning, the 16th — which should have been enough time for me to get there. After all, it had taken just two and one half days to get home from Douglas, and Hobbs was considerably closer to Washington than Douglas.

The trip to St. Louis was uneventful. But, from there on my plans began to unravel.

The agent in St. Louis told me there was a Rock Island train out of Kansas City towards Hobbs at 11:30 Sunday night. This gave me time to get in an hour's visit with an Aunt who lived not too far from the railroad station. I could have a short visit with her and still get back to the station to catch the 3:50 P.M. train for K.C. I made it back to the station in plenty of time.

However, the 3:50 didn't leave the station until 5:30. Then, after pulling out of the train shed, another 20 minutes were spent in the railroad yards admiring the beauty of the red and green switch and signal lights. Finally, things got to rolling and we reached Kansas City at 11:00 P.M.

I had sent the huge parachute bag by Railway Express through to Hobbs so I didn't have to lug it up and down crowded train car aisles and through the hordes of humanity lined up around the station platform gates.

With only the leaden B-4 bag to tote, I raced down the station concourse looking for the Rock Island 11:30 for El Paso.

Search as I could, the 11:30 P.M. Rock Island for El Paso was nowhere to be found. In desperation, I stood in line at the information counter to see if they knew where the 11:30 Rock Island train for El Paso was hidden. I finally learned the reason I couldn't find one was because there wasn't one, not that night or any other night, for that matter.

My next shot: try the bus. There was one, but it had departed at 11:00. The next one was at 7:30 Monday morning with arrival at Hobbs at 11:30 P.M. Tuesday night. That was far too close to the deadline.

Next shot: call the airport. There I found nothing available, particularly for one with no priority. The girl at the airline I talked with was very nice and, as it looked like I would be spending the night in K.C. she managed to find me a hotel room.

Last try: Check with the Air Force. This was also fruitless for two reasons: No planes headed to El Paso, the only point in the civilized world near Hobbs. And even if there had been one, they wouldn't have let me board since I didn't have a parachute. In my wisdom I had checked it to avoid lugging it on and off trains.

By now I had lost the time "cushion" I had when I departed Washington. Things now could become tight. I found the hotel the girl at the airline office had arranged for me. However, before going to bed, I consulted the Officer's Guide to see what the procedure was for reporting in late. The book suggested wiring the C.O. and advising him that you might be late in arriving. I sent the telegram and went to bed. There wasn't anything more I could do that night.

On Monday morning, the Rock Island assembled some cars and a locomotive. The cars, some of which were wooden, must have been used in the filming of "Union Pacific" and could have been around to haul Civil War troops. Once loaded, we headed towards El Paso. This was a real refugee train. All of the seats were taken and people were sitting on their bags in the aisle. Further, all the toilets were pressed into use as seats when not being used for their primary purpose.

Some twenty six hours later, by 10:30 Tuesday morning, I managed to arrive in Almagordo, New Mexico. Only about 200 miles to go and 13-1/2 hours to get it done. It was now crunch time. The only way to get to Hobbs this year was to cast my lot with the bus company. To ease my concerns, I was joined by other officers also on their way to Hobbs. Our conversation again proved that "Misery loves Company".

Ten hours after leaving Almagordo, at 11:15 P.M. Tuesday, we were deposited at the Hobbs bus station. It looked we had it made.

A 15 minute cab ride got us to the Base and signed in with 30 minutes to spare. Whew! I could have saved the cost of the telegram.

Once settled in our quarters at Hobbs we now found out how it was to be an officer. We were bunked two to a room with an Orderly to make the bed and clean up the place. Also our meals were served at tables by enlisted men. Now, this was the real Army life. Additionally, the food was as good as it had been at Dos Palos.

The first step toward learning to fly B-17 was to concentrate upon the flight manuals and attend Ground School. (One of the Ground School Instructors was a spittin' image of Jerry Cologna, the bug-eyed movie comedian and Bob Hope foil.) Ground School lasted for two weeks and was very thorough.

We were now free to leave the Base any time we felt like it — only there was one little catch. There was no place to go. Hobbs was a town of less than 10,000 souls. Among those of us who had endured Douglas, the conclusion was reached that there was a department in the Army whose sole job it was to find the worst place on earth to locate Army air bases. Our problem was; this department was doing too good a job.

Hobbs' primary claim to fame was the presence of oil fields underneath and all around it. When it came time to fly at night, this was really good fortune. The place was surrounded by many sour gas flare-offs, fires which lit the countryside and served as unmistakable beacons.

It soon became time to become acquainted with the B-17 Flying Fortress. It was huge. It seemed impossible I was going to have the chance to fly one of these great airplanes. The first opportunity to do so was a night "round robin". A "round robin" was a long (4 to 5 hours) flight which started at Hobbs, covered a route which passed over a number of cities, and landed back at Hobbs.

This first one was from Hobbs to Amarillo to Wichita Falls to Abilene to Hobbs. Eight hundred miles and over 5 hours long. The crew consisted of the Instructor Pilot, the Flight Engineer and four Student Pilots. The Student Pilots would share the left seat time. The Instructor also acted as Copilot.

Just as the Gadsden Hotel had been the center of the Douglas universe, the Harden Hotel was the center of the Hobbs universe. It had a "ballroom" featuring a tile dance floor and a juke box. Lighting was provided by several bare light bulbs suspended by their cords from the ceiling. With this decor, the word, atmosphere, pertained solely to the stuff you breathed. It goes without saying, the place also featured a bar. A well patronized bar, I must add.

Some 44 years later, 1988, Barbara and I visited Hobbs to attend a reunion of Hobbs veterans. As a part of a tour of the town, I searched out the site of the Harden Hotel. It turned out that what I found was the "site". All that remained of the venerable establishment was the tile dance floor —- everything else had been leveled. At times, progress has surprising results. I thought that the Harden would live forever. In the minds of a few who trained there, it will.

69

While we were Cadets in flight training, wives were not supposed to accompany their husbands; although some did. However, now, as officers' wives, they could. Undie's wife, Ruth, now joined him.

She managed to find a room in a home in Hobbs. With Undie now tied down, I teamed up with a new sidekick. He turned out to be H.B. Thomas, a Cadet I'd gotten to know when we were both in the same class in Advanced at Douglas. H.B. (H = Halcott) was from California; thus, he and I had quite a few things in common. Among them were a similar sense of humor and a spirit for adventure. A mighty good pair it turned out to be.

The presence of Ruth slowed down Undie a bit. However, Ruth, Undie, H.B. and I soon became a regular Harden Hotel foursome. With three to chose from, Ruth never lacked for a dancing partner. However, all too frequently Undie would get a load on and disappear leaving Ruth with H.B. and me. When the evening came to an end and Undie was nowhere in sight, it fell to H.B. and me to escort Ruth home. Never, did either H.B. or I escort her without the other. We figured in that way neither of us would be tempted to take advantage of the situation. A very reasonable and prudent precaution since, from an available girl standpoint, Hobbs was far worse than Douglas. And Douglas was bad enough.

We were kept busy flying. It was almost never just a short one or two hour's flight. It was mostly "round robins" in all kinds of weather and at any conceivable hour. To quote from one of the letters home:

> "I flew 16 hours out of 24 which is pretty rough. For 10 hours of that I never saw the ground. We took off at 2:00 A.M. and circled the field above an overcast until 7:30 A.M. —- pretty tiresome. Then we paired off with another ship and climbed to 18,000 feet for a little high altitude formation. Then we flew a round robin..... like this: Hobbs to Kansas City to Omaha to Denver to Hobbs, nonstop. We got back over Hobbs

at 11:30 A.M. only to find the field closed in with fog. And no airports open that could be reached by our dwindling gas supply. — it looked like we were going to become Caterpillars. [Bail out] Fortunately, the ceiling lifted to 300 feet and we landed after several attempts, at 1:00 P.M."

(At the time this was written, the attempt was to impress upon the folks what kind of a really hot shot Pilot their son had become. In all probability, it succeeded in scaring the day lights out of them.)

On most of the "round robins" four Student Pilots would be sent up in one airplane with a Flight Engineer but no Instructor Pilot. First Pilot and Copilot time was to be shared equally among the four. This meant that at any given time two Students had nothing to do. Standing behind the Pilot and Copilot seats while the other Students were flying was a bore, so the usual practice for the non-flying Students was to go back to the radio room and lie down on the floor and grab some sack time.

One night such a group was up flying. The Pilot and Copilot were not paying much attention to what was happening outside. Suddenly, the Pilot looked up and confused some stars for an airplane on a collision course. To avoid what appeared to be an imminent head on "collision," he "dumped" the nose of the airplane. Quickly, he realized it was not an airplane after all and proceeded to haul back on the control column. All this thrashing about had no big effect upon the Pilot and Copilot since they had their seat belts fastened. However, the two Students asleep in the radio room were not belted in. When the Pilot put the airplane into a dive, this action succeeded in suspending the two Students about 3 or 4 feet in the air. Then, when he pulled the plane into a steep recovery, the floor of the radio room came up to meet the two airborne Students with more than a little force. Result: one Student with a couple of cracked ribs and one with a number of bruises. This incident made sleeping on the radio room floor less popular.

71

One of the Hobbs Instructor Pilots was an Aeronautical Engineer. After considerable calculation, he concluded it was possible to loop a B-17 without inflicting any structural damage to it. One day he decided to put his theory to proof. He was successful; he looped it. However, this was too good of a secret to be kept forever. Someone, either the Instructor, the Copilot or the Flight Engineer had to brag about it. Once the secret was out, the aircraft involved was immediately grounded and thoroughly inspected. No damage could be found. However, the Instructor was dismissed from the Service. Rumor was he then went to work for Boeing as a test Pilot.

One weekend, H.B. and I decided to search out the surrounding territory for some different scenery. We settled upon Carlsbad and its famous caverns, only about a 2 hour bus ride from Hobbs. We got to the city of Carlsbad and decided to investigate it a bit before taking in the caverns.

Somehow or other, our wanderings about resulted in meeting the daughter of the Mayor of the City of Carlsbad.

In our conversation, we learned that she was planning a party for the Saturday afternoon and evening. Result: we were invited. Being reasonably sure that the caverns very likely would still be there on Sunday, H.B. and I accepted the invitation.

The girl's father, not too long before this time, had lost his wife and, fortunately for us, he was out of town. The party was to be held in his apartment which was located over some store or other in downtown Carlsbad. It wound up being quite a celebration. The featured drink was a "pink lady" —- a new one for H.B. and me. Later, we discovered a "pink lady" was straight grain alcohol flavored and colored with a small amount of strawberry syrup. Man,

**B-17 PILOT TRAINING CLASS, HOBBS, NEW MEXICO
MIDDLE ROW, 8TH AND 9TH FROM LEFT: H.B.
THOMAS AND THE AUTHOR, RESP.**

was it potent!! And could it deliver a headache!! Needless to say, H.B. and I didn't make the Caverns on Sunday. It was a monumental accomplishment for us just to get back to Hobbs. That was the first and last time H.B. and I attempted an expedition to Carlsbad or its caverns.

Flying continued at a heavy pace. Soon it became time for the final check ride.

The Instructor Pilot had me take off. Of course, just as we lifted off he pulled #1 engine throttle and yelled "Engine Failure". This had been expected, was handled with little problem and received a "Well done". We climbed on out and got some altitude. There followed the usual power on and power off stalls, procedure turns and other routine maneuvers. Finally, the Instructor said, "Put it in the steepest bank you can." Well, this was certainly an invitation to show how good I was. So, I stood the thing on its right wing tip. About the time I got it racked up good and tight and was straining to hold it there, the Instructor pulled the throttles off on #3 and #4!! We almost rolled onto our back as I struggled to put in full left rudder, crank on full left aileron and get the nose down. As I wrestled with the controls, the Instructor calmly pulled off #1 and #2 throttles and said, "Now, straighten the thing out, drop the nose and slowly bring the two 'good' engines back up in power."

That little exercise taught me a lot in a short period of time. That is, "How to handle the loss of two engines on one side" and "Never, repeat, never turn into one or two dead engines." This knowledge would come in very, very handy a few months later.

Before we knew it, our training was completed. It was now time to head for a replacement depot. There, we would be assigned our crew members and sent on to a Combat Crew Training Base. We were told that we were being transferred to the replacement depot in Salt Lake City.

CHAPTER 8
THE REPLACEMENT DEPOTS

It was time to board the train and move. Lucky once more, we got Pullman cars.

When first assigned to Hobbs, I had discovered the hard way that it was nearly impossible to get there by train. In fact, I didn't; I got there by bus. We now found out it was almost impossible to get out of there by train. We left on Monday morning, March 27, 1944. After a day and one half of traveling, we reached Clovis, New Mexico only 200 miles north of Hobbs. Two hundred net miles in thirty six hours equals just over 5 miles per hour!! However, we had really traveled a great deal more than 200 miles. We left Hobbs headed southwest to El Paso (about 200 miles); then we headed east northeast 400 miles to Abilene, Texas; from there we traveled some 250 miles northwest to Clovis. Clovis is 200 miles north of Hobbs. In our wanderings we had been west, south, east and north of Hobbs.

From Clovis, we went in a generally north-west direction through northern New Mexico, southern and western Colorado. After winding through the Royal Gorge, which was most spectacular, we reached Salt Lake City on Thursday morning, March 30, 1944.

The facilities at Salt Lake City were minimal. The barracks were heated with coal and the result was a pall of acrid coal smoke which seemed to engulf the area continuously. We were told the Base was about to be closed and, if not assigned within two weeks, we probably would be sent to another Replacement Depot.

The Base routine consisted of a roll call at 7:30 A.M. and another one at 1:00 P.M., period. Nothing else happened, except we got our shots brought up to date, as was needed.

It didn't take long to learn that the smarter ones assigned to the replacement pool lived in town in hotel rooms and commuted to the Base for the roll calls. Ruth, Undie's wife, had gone back to Montana from Hobbs. So Undie joined H.B. and me in taking a room (#202) in the Carlton Hotel. This was a small new hotel not very far from Temple Square. Since it was a new hotel and commercial business was not very brisk, we were most welcome. After all, someone had to pay the mortgage. In fact, I don't remember the hotel management ever saying a word to any of us concerning our oft times very boisterous conduct.

It didn't take us long to figure out a routine. Get up (at the hotel) around 6:30 A.M. Have breakfast at a nearby restaurant. Grab a cab to the Base. On the trip to the Base, the three of us would all flip a coin with the "odd man" being the loser. The loser's duty was to stand the 7:30 A.M. roll call for all three of us. We knew each others' serial numbers. So, if the response to roll call was challenged, the correct serial number reply could be given.

On arrival at the Base, the coin toss loser would head for roll call and the two winners would immediately head for the assigned barracks and the sack. The third member would also hit the bed as soon as roll call was over. The three of us would stay in the sack until 12:30 P.M. We all would stand the 1:00 P.M. roll call. After that we would grab a cab back to the hotel and go back to bed until 4:30 P.M. Then, get cleaned up; have dinner; go out on the town until all activity ceased or we became incapable of activity. Whoever said war was hell didn't have Salt Lake City duty.

In respect to the importance of the roll call, about the only important information I can remember being passed at any of the roll calls was to request we not hang around the high schools waiting for the girls to get out of school. For those who had not thought of this girl finding technique, this was welcome info. For those who didn't need this intelligence, it was humorous. Undie, H.B. and I thought this to be needless info.

One night there were about 5 of us, all from Douglas, walking down the street. Then, what should happen? We ran into Lt. Rosen, our old nemesis from Douglas. We surrounded him and engaged him in close conversation. Some of the questions concerning operations at Douglas directed at the Lieutenant were a little less than friendly. Soon, we could see that he was getting worried. He was not very big and the 5 of us were all pretty good sized. Further, he had the same rank as we had; thus, he couldn't resort to rank to extricate himself. He thought retribution was about to be delivered. After he had sweated a while, we stepped back and bid him a cheerful good bye. However, the release was with the admonition that the next time he runs into a group from Douglas, that group might not be so understanding and friendly as we. Therefore, it was strongly suggested he carry this thought back to Douglas and perhaps change his conduct.

Although there were about 4,000 officers at the Base, Salt Lake City was a Serviceman's paradise. I believe if H.B. and I decided we wanted to date a blond and a brunette in a 1939 Chevy for the evening, we probably could have gone out and stood on the sidewalk to wait for that combination to come by. And very shortly that combination would arrive, honk, wave, smile and stop. From there on it would be up to us.

While Undie shared the room in the Carlton with H.B. and me, he almost always went his separate way. We all did a fair amount of drinking; however, Undie did more than his share with the result he frequently had a rather heavy load on.

It was this latter tendency of Undie's which led to one very interesting and somewhat frustrating evening for H.B. and me.

H.B. and I had become acquainted with a couple of girls. We thought it might be a good idea to have the girls up to the room for an evening of conversation and learned discussion. On the afternoon of the chosen day on the way in from the Base, we suggested to Undie he might want to find other quarters for all or the major portion of the evening. Both H.B. and I thought he understood and agreed.

Before meeting the girls, H.B. and I stopped by the room to tidy it up for the main event which was to follow. As we started to straighten things up, we were greeted by the sight of Undie, clad only in his shorts, passed out on one of the beds. This posed somewhat of a dilemma for H.B. and me. After a little quick thinking, a solution was devised. Some friends had room #302 directly above. Why not move Undie up there? The key to #302 was quickly gotten from the desk. Then, one of us took Undie's shoulders and the other his feet and we carried him out of our room up the back stairs and deposited him on a bed in #302.

We tidied up our room and left to pick up the girls and take them to dinner. After dinner, the suggestion to go to our hotel room was accepted without hesitation. So, back to the hotel we went.

In great anticipation we entered the room where anticipation suddenly turned to consternation. The place looked like a tornado had been through it.

It seemed that while H.B., the girls and I had been at dinner, Undie had come to. Since the surroundings in #302 were very similar to our room he went on a search for his clothes only to find none of the clothing would fit. His foggy condition didn't help his thinking processes. However, it finally dawned upon him that he was in the wrong room. His immediate problem became how to get back to the right room. Not too easy, since he had on only his shorts and had no key. A phone call and the desk clerk got him to #202 and reunited with his clothes. By this time, however, he was more than a bit unhappy. Recalling what H.B. and I were up to and figuring we had placed him in his predicament, he decided to wreck the room —- an operation he accomplished with considerable thoroughness. So, H.B.'s and my idea for a great evening was dashed. In spite of our deep disappointment, our friendship with Undie withstood the test.

In later incidents we found that Undie's unconscious presence didn't dampen the spirit of the evening's activities at all.

Utah bordered on prohibition. Booze was sold only through state owned stores of which there were 4 in Salt Lake City. Booze by the drink was not served at all. In order to have a drink with a meal it was necessary for you to bring your own bottle. The restaurant would serve you ice and mixer, for a small consideration. To further curb the consumption of alcohol, they had in place a rationing system. This allowed one fifth of whisky per month per person, which was woefully inadequate for our operations.

It did not take long to figure out how to circumvent this nonsense. Apparently there was no central clearing house to check on the issuance of ration cards. Thus, all it took was a trip to each of the four stores to sign up for a ration card. This action immediately quadrupled the supply. Then, to further negate this legal "silliness", whenever someone was transferred out, it was clearly understood his ration card/s would be left behind. Thus, the supply of booze was limited only by the supply of money.

Our base pay was $130/month. If you flew at least 4 hours in the calendar month, an additional $65 was added to it. The life style we were leading began to eat into what little reserves we had.

On April 15th, our Salt Lake City cash problem was erased. The Salt Lake City Replacement Depot was being closed. We were put on a troop train to be delivered to the Replacement Depot at Lincoln, Nebraska. This trip introduced us to the discomforts of the specially built troop transport cars. Based upon the design for a box car, they contained as many 3 high stacks of bunks that could be fit within. There were rudimentary sanitary facilities, but no sitting or lounge area. No one should be surprised that the usual name applied to the "Troop Transport Cars" was "Cattle Cars."

In due course we arrived at the Lincoln Replacement Depot. It was snowing (the wet kind), the place was encased in a cloud of coal smoke as bad as Salt Lake and the ground was a sea of gooey black mud. It soon became apparent that the laxity of the Salt Lake City operation had not been put on the train with us. Once more, we were back in the ARMY! We could only go into town after 5:00 P.M., but we were required to be back on Base by midnight. Although, an hour or two tardiness carried no penalty. Much more than that was asking for trouble.

Unfortunately, as at Salt Lake City, there was nothing, other than the two roll calls, to do on the Base. So time really dragged.

Because of the excesses in Salt Lake City, the cash situation had become so dire that I was forced to send a telegram home requesting $40 for "summer uniforms".

While we were somewhat restrained, we did avail ourselves to several evenings in town. These excursions introduced us to a new, to us, alcoholic beverage. Gluck's STITE. It looked like a dark beer. It had a taste similar to beer. However, it had twice the alcohol content of beer, a fact which was duly noted on the label.

As a rule, we did not read labels. So, on our second encounter with STITE we were really blindsided. As we groped our way back to Base, it was obvious we needed to odd man to see which one would stand the 8:00 A.M. roll call. There was no need for all three of us to suffer. H.B. and I "won" the toss.

About 8:00 A.M. the next morning, I was vaguely aware of someone shaking my bed.I suggested he not do that. The next thing

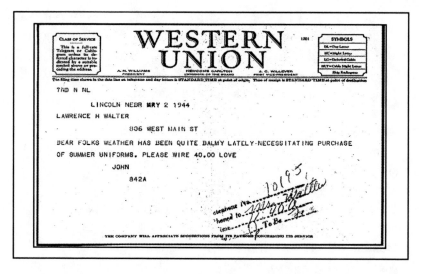

I felt was the foot of my cot being lifted a foot or so into the air and released for a free fall to the floor. This did not improve my condition or attitude at all.

The "voice" requested my name, rank and serial number. I informed him: "Read the damn tag on the end of the damned cot. And leave me the Hell alone!!"

Now it was my turn to be informed: "Lieutenant, I am the Adjutant and you had better get your ass out of that sack and get it over to Headquarters, pronto!"

At Headquarters, H.B. and I were made aware that we were required to attend roll calls in person; and to impress this fact upon us, the C.O. told us we were confined to Base until shipped out. H.B. and I came to the conclusion that Lincoln was not all that great, after all. We didn't care if we never got to go into town again.

We spent the remaining evenings in Lincoln around the pot bellied stove in the barracks. Although we could no longer enjoy the pleasures of downtown Lincoln, we were fortunate in that friends managed to keep us supplied with liquid refreshments.

While H.B. and I were reflecting upon the errors of our ways, we discovered we both had a gum problem. The first, and most horrifying, thought: TRENCH MOUTH!! DAMN THAT SALT LAKE CITY! We decided a visit to the dentist was called for. The resulting conversation went something like this:

Me: "What have I got, Doctor?"
Dentist: "Hmmmm. I've got to check some of my books. I've never seen this."
Me: "How bad is it, Sir?"
Dentist: "Where have you been stationed, Lieutenant?"
Me: "Salt Lake City, Sir."
Dentist: "Don't they have fresh fruit and vegetables there?"
Me: "Yes, I guess so, Sir."
Dentist: "I seriously recommend you begin eating some."
Me: "Will that cure trench mouth, Sir?"
Dentist: "Lieutenant, you do not have trench mouth. You have the beginnings of scurvy. You had better get to eating some fresh fruit and vegetables pretty quick or you won't have any teeth left to eat anything with."
Me: "Thank you, Sir, I'll do just that."

It seemed our Salt Lake City diet of meat, eggs, fried potatoes and booze did not contain much vitamin C. Once we corrected our diet deficiencies, in a short time, the malady passed with no trace. Our eating habits now included this sage advice: "Be sure to have orange juice with the booze. And don't forget to order a big salad with that steak and French fries."

Then, came the word. We had been assigned our Crew. First, I met Tom Sevald, Copilot, and John Ingleman, Bombardier. I was told that, as there was a shortage of Navigators, the Navigator would join us at our Crew Training Base which would be Dyersburg, Tennessee. Dyersburg is about 60-70 miles due north of Memphis. H.B. and his crew were also assigned to Dyersburg. Undie had yet to be assigned.

Next, I met the rest of the Crew: Jimmie Cunningham, Engineer: Jim Purdy, Assistant Engineer; Larry Franceschina, Jack Sheets and Don Baldwin, Gunners; and Bob Kiefer, Radio Operator. They all seemed to be a real good bunch of guys.

On May 13, 1944, we boarded a troop train and left for Dyersburg, Tennessee. We were more than ready to go. The month's sojourn in Lincoln had about driven H.B. and me up the wall.

On the portion of the trip from Kansas City to St. Louis, H.B. and I rode in the caboose with the Conductor and Rear End Brakeman. This was much better accommodation than the "cattle cars" we had drawn for the trip.

CHAPTER 9
CREW TRAINING

We arrived at Dyersburg in the middle of May, resplendent in our nice warm woolen winter uniforms. The temperature must have been in the 80's and the humidity at least equal to that, and we were dripping with sweat and on the verge of a heat stroke.

The Lincoln PX had very little uniform stock, either winter or summer. So, we had not been able to purchase the summer essentials before arriving in Dyersburg. This situation was soon remedied. A few of the fellows went all the way and bought the whole summer uniform outfit. This included the Class "A" uniform which was made up of the tropical worsted wool blouse and the accompanying trousers, service cap and a host of the other little details. On the other hand, there were those, such as I, who figured two sets of Class "B's" (trousers and shirt only) in both tropical worsted and cotton would suffice. Fresh from the Salt Lake "experience", that was all I could afford. Further adding to my financial woes brought about by excessive spending in Salt Lake City was the fact that I now had gone two months without flight pay.

My decision, while mainly driven by monetary reasons, also involved two other factors. I was pretty sure that our next station after Dyersburg would be England. Even though I knew little about England, I was pretty sure the need for summer uniforms there would be near zero. Then, there was the frequency with which we were moved around. There was no point in getting any more stuff to tote than absolutely necessary.

Tom, our Copilot, and I hit it off real well. He had graduated from single engine advanced, so it was up to me to acquaint and train him with the mind boggling intricacies of the B-17. I recalled some advice we had been given at Hobbs, which was, "You'll probably get some disappointed Fighter Pilot To Be as a Copilot. The best thing for you to do is to let him know that he can have number 4 throttle as his own. Then tell him to make like that is a fighter plane throttle and to fly formation with you."

Tom was eager to learn and took the whole thing very seriously. In fact, he took life as a whole very seriously, however, he did have a dry, quiet sense of humor. Our social interests were quite different. He'd rather read a book or have an in-depth discussion than go to the Officers' Club and nurse a beer with the guys. Tom was from a strong Catholic family in Royal Oak, Michigan.

John, our Bombardier, and I also hit it off quite well. John was from Champaign-Urbana, Illinois. Our social interests were somewhat similar; however, he was married, a fact which limited our shared off-base activities. I met his wife, Vivian, when she came to visit on one occasion. A really warm and nice person.

Among the originally assigned enlisted crew, only Jim Purdy, Assistant Engineer, was married. He was from eastern Ohio and was a pleasant and out-going person. The glint in his eyes suggested some otherwise hidden inclinations toward mischievousness.

Larry Franceschina was from San Francisco and he had had some college. He was a real extrovert, a deal maker, a girl "magnet" and a budding entrepreneur.

Jack Sheets was from Oklahoma. He was quiet and sharp. His comments and replies always were well studied before being delivered.

As it turned out, during our training at Dyersburg, we would lose three of the originally assigned enlisted crew.

The first to be replaced was Jimmie Cunningham, Engineer, who was replaced by Jim McCue. I did not have time to become well acquainted with Jimmie.

McCue had been held over from a previous class due to illness. Thus, he had gone through some of the training which now lay ahead of us. Jim was a red-headed Irishman. From Iowa, as I recall. He was a shy and quiet person. I think he was either in awe of or intimidated by me or my rank. Why this was, I have no idea.

The other crew members to be replaced were Baldwin, Gunner, and Kiefer, Radio Operator. Kiefer was not replaced until the very end of our training. Both were replaced because of acute and chronic airsickness.

The May weather in Tennessee was a real pain. Air conditioning was only for the movies. As I recall, none of the buildings I was in at Dyersburg had air conditioning. As the saying goes, "It's not the heat it's the humidity" was right on the button for Dyersburg. After taking a shower, it was almost impossible to get dried off. The mere effort of using the towel to dry yourself was enough exertion to cause the perspiration to flow, ensuring that you remained dripping wet.

Flying in the mid Mississippi Valley under 10,000 feet in the middle of summer is not the smoothest ride in the world — especially in the afternoon, when the fair weather cumulus begin to appear. They bring with them a lot of strong up and down drafts. Couple the "bumpy air" with high temperature and high humidity, and you have made-to-order conditions for airsickness.

Both Baldwin and Kiefer usually upchucked (more descriptively, "flashed their hash") every time we flew in anything except the smoothest air. They spent more time at cleaning out the airplane than at any other single activity, except, worrying about being air sick on the next flight.

Baldwin was replaced by George Hasselback whose home town was in Michigan. He not only could operate radios but other things. He was a real party person with a great sense of humor and a perpetual smile.

Finally, about a week after getting to Dyersburg I was back in the air. I had been on the ground for about two months, since the last flight at Hobbs. Naturally, before entrusting the lives of nine others in my hands, a check ride was prescribed. It turned out that the Check Pilot for this flight was Captain Bragg.

Few books or articles about a B-17 are ever printed without a picture of a B-17 flying along with a huge gash almost all the way through the fuselage just ahead of the tail. It looks like the airplane's fuselage is almost cut in two. The gash was caused by the wing of a German Me109. The B-17 flew long enough to land but never to fly again. The 109 didn't survive. Captain Bragg was the Pilot who brought that airplane home.

(Just a few years ago, Captain Bragg's name would come up again. During a conversation with my next door neighbor, Henry Abts, who was also an Army Air Force Pilot, mentioned that he had received a letter from "the" Captain Bragg. It turned out he and Bragg had been in the same Cadet class. Another example of a Small World.)

I passed the flight check, and we then began to fly and train as a crew.

The first of June our Navigator, Nelson Kurz, arrived, fresh out of Pan American Airways Coral Gables, Florida Navigation School.

He was a serious and studious fellow from the Bronx whose biggest non-flying interest was how to make money.

For the crew members whose stations were ahead of the bomb bay, the usual entrance to the airplane was through the forward escape hatch. To enter, you grabbed the door frame at the top of the hatch opening and swung your feet up into the opening and pulled yourself on into the airplane. Being short of stature, Nelson could not reach the door frame without a pretty good jump. However, when he did manage to get a grip of the door frame, he did not have the necessary arm and shoulder strength to complete the movement. The result was he had to enter the airplane through the rear door and walk forward the length of the airplane. I'm sure this bothered him considerably.

The Dyersburg Base was constructed to create the illusion of an English air base. Of course, the barracks and other buildings were standard U.S. Government issue. However, the streets bore English names and the runway was not the nice level kind which we had become accustomed to out West. It was a new experience to use a runway having a mild resemblance to a roller coaster.

The training consisted of ground school and flying. Flying was done both as individual aircraft and as a part of a formation. We had both day and night practice bombing in which we used 100 pound practice bombs. These were rather thin steel casings which were filled with sand to give them the needed weight. The tail of the bomb, in addition to the guiding fins, was fitted with a small explosive charge which gave off a flash of light and a puff of white smoke on bomb impact. This explosive charge made it possible to see where the bombs hit either during the day or at night.

The target consisted of a bull's eye marked on the ground. At night it was outlined with flare pots. The airplane carried a camera which was aimed at the ground. When the bombs were dropped, the camera started and took a series of pictures. These photos provided a means to see how good or bad we were. John was pretty good. Thus, we, as a crew, were also pretty good.

On occasion, we were sent up to build up time and to practice inter crew communications and activities. By and large this was pretty boring. So, somewhere along the line the party needed to be spiced up a bit. There were three activities which came to be as a result of this training boredom.

One of these was to "check the Mississippi". Naturally, the only way this could be done adequately was to get down close to the river. The drill was to fly along the river at an altitude which would put the aircraft below the tops of the trees lining the river. At this altitude, given the torturous nature of the river, it was quite easy for a rather noisy B-17 to sneak up on anyone on or near the river. The person most often surprised was a fisherman, half asleep, drifting along in his rowboat. As a B-17 came around a bend in the river and roared straight at him at 160 miles per hour and 50 feet or so above the river, his first and only reaction was to leap overboard.

It was well understood by all Pilots engaged in this practice that this "inspection" could only be done from north to south. A mid air collision at 50 feet over the river would be spectacular; however, it would leave no survivors. The crew enjoyed this sport. John and Nelson, in the nose, could catch the guy's terrified expression before he went overboard. The fellows in the rear could report upon the end of the event.

Another sport required the "cooperation" of the Navy. Just north of Memphis was a Naval Air Station, Millington NAS. This was a primary flight training base which used Stearmans. Our sport was to come up behind a formation of a half dozen "Yellow Perils", dive down underneath them and pull up in front and above them. This really stirred up the air just ahead of their formation. The result was Stearmans all over the sky.

During a session at the Officers' Club one day, someone mentioned the seemingly brave farmer who plowed his field at the end of the active runway. We were very "concerned" that he was not aware of the danger which exists at the end of an active runway. After some discussion, it was decided that in order for him to appreciate his peril, he should be shown a B-17 up good and close. Maybe he then would develop a better appreciation of the danger. It was concluded the best time to do this would be if he happened to be plowing during a formation takeoff. In formation takeoff, there was a spacing of about 20 seconds between airplanes. H.B., another Pilot, Gene Peterson, and I decided to provide the obviously needed instruction for this careless tiller of the soil. As we three were scattered through the formation, this would greatly enhance our plan.

Sure enough, when the next formation flight came along, the farmer was out chugging along on his tractor. The Pilot of the first airplane of the "educational team" held it down on the deck after takeoff. Due to the tractor's engine noise, the farmer didn't hear the B-17 coming until it was right on him. As with the fisherman on the Mississippi, the farmer's first reaction was to jump —- which he did just as the first airplane passed low overhead. He didn't take time to shut off the engine or put the transmission in neutral. He just jumped.

By the time the driver had picked himself up and caught up with and gotten back on the tractor, here came the second "team" member. Again, it was tractor bail out time which was followed by a repeat of the get up, chase down and climb on operation. When the third "team" member came over, the farmer had given up; he and his tractor were at the edge of the field heading for the barn.

We never saw the farmer again. It was most obvious that our course in air field safety had been very effective.

Tom's, John's and Nelson's extra curricular interests were different from mine. In view of this circumstance, I continued my off duty friendship with H.B. H.B.'s crew, with the exception of his Copilot,

"Red" Salvo, had the same interests as H.B. and I. Thus, H.B., his Bombardier and Navigator and I became a foursome for off-the-base activities. Those rounding out the foursome, were Dave Webber and Charlie Roan, H.B.'s Bombardier and Navigator, respectively. What made this group something to be reckoned with was the fact that Charlie Roan drove a Buick Roadmaster (top of the line) four door convertible!! Put the top down on that automobile and put four young Air Force officers in it and "Look out, Girls!!"

As a social center, Dyersburg struck out. However, that made little difference to the four of us since we were mobile, on Charlie Roan's wheels. Our excursions led us to Memphis and the Peabody Hotel to the south, and to Paducah and the Irving S. Cobb Hotel to the north. Our preference was Paducah —- primarily because there were no Navy types and few other military personnel anywhere near there. We made quite a few trips to Paducah. One member of the group, for reasons which can not be related here, was given the nickname, "The Duke of Paducah", after one of these trips.

It was on one of the excursions to Paducah that another one of the fellows, who shall be nameless, became involved in a situation which was more than a little embarrassing for him. It seems as if the girl who was with him in the car was having trouble finding something in her purse. Finally, in desperation, she dumped the contents of her purse in the most convenient place available, his lap. This, in itself, was no big deal; however, when she did so, the covers on a couple of lipsticks came off. The result was a number of very pronounced lipstick smears on the front of his tan slacks. He spent the rest of our stay in Paducah either in the dark or with his hands held over the front of his pants. No matter how he attempted to explain the way the lipstick got there, the efforts received only loud and disbelieving laughter.

Since it was quite probable we would, in the not too distant future, be required to fly to England, we were sent off on both single and multiplane navigation/bombing missions. The "bombing" missions consisted of taking pictures of the "target" and were usually flown

91

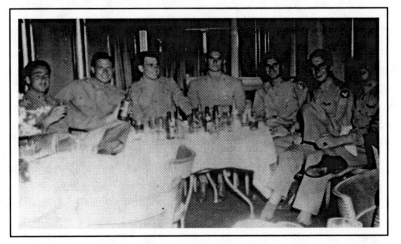

THE PEABODY HOTEL, MEMPHIS, TENNESSEE

Left to Right: Gene Peterson, The Author, Dave Webber, Charlie Roan, "Red" Salvo, unknown, H.B. Thomas

at around 20,000 feet altitude. Some of the "targets" were Evansville's Republic Aircraft Plant, the St. Louis Union Station and Louisville's Bowman Field.

Early single plane navigational flights had raised some doubt about Nelson's navigating ability. As a result, I requested permission to fly an extra mission. We decided upon a night single plane "round robin" to Louisville; Charleston, West Virginia; Knoxville, Tennessee; Jackson, Mississippi and back to Dyersburg. The aim of the exercise, of course, was to give Nelson a chance to use and hone his celestial and other navigation skills.

For the first portion of the trip and until we got to Jackson, Mississippi Tom and I used pilotage and the radio compass to keep track of our position. Nelson had hit everything on the nose up to that point. With that accomplished, I reasoned he certainly could find Dyersburg since it was an easy shot from Jackson. Tom and I relaxed, turned on the auto pilot, switched the radio compass to the commercial band and tuned in some good popular music. It was just a question of a little time and soon we would be home.

I had an idea about how long it should take us to get back to the Base. A few minutes after that time had passed, I called Nelson on the intercom and asked him, "How goes it?"; his reply, "I need to take another star shot, Sir." Thinking that I might have under estimated the time from Jackson to Dyersburg, I decided not to push him. More time passed. I repeated my earlier question. His reply was the same. I decided, "One more chance." More time passed. The earlier dialog was repeated a third time. Being no immediate response, my next question was, "Are you lost?"; reply, "I think so, Sir."

There was one problem with that question. It should have been "Are WE lost?" By now Tom and I, had lost track of our position.

Now it was tighten up the ship time. How much fuel do we have?

Next, change the radio compass from the commercial frequency band to the radio range frequency band. Pull engine power back, and lean out the engine fuel mixture. We needed to save fuel. Check the crew to be sure their parachutes were close at hand. No unnecessary conversation on the intercom. It was "pucker" time for all on board.

We soon picked up a radio range signal. Even with my halting ability with Morse code, I could determine it was the St. Louis radio range. We were at least 200 miles beyond Dyersburg. However, I didn't know whether we were south, east or north of the station; thus, it was necessary to fly an orientation on the St. Louis range station to find out where we were in relation to it. Completion of this procedure revealed that we were in the southeast quadrant of the St. Louis radio range. We turned to a heading for the Base where we landed about 2 hours late.

I was amazed at the effusive, "Boy, are we glad to see you home safe," greeting. Then I found out why the warm greeting. The Radio

Operator, of course, had heard the intercom conversation concerning "lost", "fuel level" and "parachutes". He had given these words his own interpretation, and then, without my knowing it, he had radioed the Base that we were lost, running out of fuel and we would soon be bailing out. I got the R.O. off to one side and in rather plain, strong language instructed him to "NEVER, REPEAT, NEVER send a radio message without clearing it with me first. UNDERSTOOD?" It never happened again. Although the replacement of Kiefer by Hasselback occurred shortly after, it was not related to this event.

This little incident led to the selection of Nelson's nickname, "COLUMBUS". I tried to have him replaced; however, I was told no replacement was available. While not fully explored, I believe that the reason Columbus did not get lost on the first legs of our flight was the result of him "following" Tom's and my radio navigation path.

The other Pilots around the Base reminded me very often about this little happening. It was the first time I'd gotten lost. Of course, this favorite saying of pilots takes care of these occasions. "I was not lost, I was just in doubt of my position."

Our training up to this time had given the Pilots, the Bombardier and the Navigator an opportunity to show off their skills. It was now time for the Gunners to do their thing. However, western Tennessee was not the place to go flying around shooting real live bullets out of 50 caliber machine guns. We were sent off to the Gulf of Mexico for this training. We flew from Dyersburg to Mobile, Alabama and landed at the Air Base there to pick up the ammunition and load the guns. The guns loaded, we took off and flew out over the Gulf for gunnery practice.

The first guns to be fired were the ones in the top turret. With the guns pointing forward and level, McCue let fire with a short burst. Tom and I thought we'd been shot. When the turret is in that position, the ends of the gun barrels are only about 18 inches above the Pilot's and Copilot's heads. The airplane structure did little to block the muzzle blast and noise. The concussions shook dust and dirt loose from every nook and cranny of the cockpit. After the initial surprise, it was interesting to feel the aircraft react as the various guns were fired. After the firing was completed, we headed back to Mobile and landed so the guns could be cleared and any left over ammunition removed from the airplane.

After we landed, we were led in from the end of the runway and parked by the "Follow Me" jeep and the ramp crew. When it came time to leave, we realized we had been parked too close to the hanger. There was not enough room to turn either to the right or left without a wing tip hitting the hanger. We had picked up an Instructor Pilot from Dyersburg to ride as Copilot on the way back to Base. He said I better call the tower and have them send a tug to push us back far enough so we could turn without hitting the hanger. After making a request for the tug we were told that it was going to take quite a while since the base personnel didn't know where to find a tow bar to fit a B-17.

In some of our Officers' Club "flying" sessions I had heard it was possible to back up a B-17. Now it was my turn to be the Instructor. I told the Instructor we really didn't need to wait for a tug. I would back us up far enough to get turning clearance. He was skeptical, but either he wanted to learn something new or witness a young Pilot making a fool of himself, because he didn't try to persuade me otherwise. Of course, while trying not to show it, I wasn't too sure, myself, since I had never done it.

We started the engines and let them warm up. Now was the time. Unlock the tail wheel. Lock the right main wheel brake. Release the left main wheel brake. Push the control column forward a little bit. Advance #4 engine throttle. Sure enough. As #4 engine increased in power the tail rose slightly which allowed the tail wheel to go into caster and the left wing moved backward as the airplane pivoted around the right main. The procedure was repeated several times alternating between #4 and #1 engines and the brakes on the right and left mains. The operation produced a backward duck-like waddle movement. The B-17 could be backed up!! Wait 'till the next Officers' Club session!! Soon we had enough clearance to turn the airplane and head out for take off.

The Instructor's comments were: "That's a little hard on engines and tires." He couldn't avoid smiling when he said it, and I've often wondered how soon after he, too, tried it.

Dyersburg is about 250 miles from Washington so, I had been working on Mother and Dad to come down and visit. Finally, I talked them into doing so. Mary Jane came with them.

When he started work with the Baltimore and Ohio railroad, Dad, as did all of the other railroad employees, kept a time book. In this book were recorded the hours worked each day. It came naturally to also use this time book as a sort of diary to record all kinds of important events.

The details of the folk's trip were covered in Dad's time book entry like this:

"June 25: Left at 8 a.m. for Dyersburg, Tenn. to see John. Arrived at 4 p.m. Stayed at the Cordell Hull Hotel. Visited Air Field and inspected B-17 Flying Fortress. Took dinner at the Mess Hall. Left 6/28, 2 p.m. arrived home 10 p.m. 540 miles round trip."

Before their trip down I had managed to get a single plane night flight which could be slightly and unofficially altered to include Washington. So that the citizens of that fair city could be made aware of our presence, we dropped down to about 500 feet AGL (above ground level), set all four props into high RPM, turned on the landing lights and flew the 22 block length of Main Street from its western end to its eastern end. We WERE noticed. Again, Dad's time book:

"June 20, John flew over here in a B-17."

It was time to move on again. We realized we were getting closer to the shooting war. In fact, we should soon be in it.

On July 20th, we left Dyersburg with a seven day delay en route to Kearney, Nebraska. I headed straight for home in Washington.

While home I decided to have a check up by Dr. Charlie Smiley, our family dentist. In the course of our conversation, I asked how his daughter, Barbara, was doing in Chicago. Barbara and I had gone through high school in the same class. Although we had never dated, we had been involved in a number of the same social and school activities. Before I knew it, I decided to leave for Kearney a few days early and make a stop over in Chicago. As it turned out, that visit had a great effect upon my life.

CHAPTER 10
HEADING OVERSEAS

On July 29, 1944, Crew #5442 reassembled at the Kearney, Nebraska Army Air Base. We knew this was just a temporary stop. At the present, where we would go from here was the big unknown. Would it be east to Europe or Africa? Would it be west to the Pacific?

At this time in the War, almost of all of the B-17's were being used in the European Theater of Operations. This fact took some of the uncertainty out of the situation. The Kearney Army Air Base field was covered with brand new B-17's. We were soon assigned one of these bright, shiny airplanes. It was a Boeing B-17G, serial number 43-38286.

Our first assignment was to thoroughly check out the plane both on the ground and in the air. Since our necks were going to be at risk, it was unnecessary for the Base personnel to emphasize that we direct our closest attention to the smallest of details. Singled out for particular scrutiny were the magnetic and flux gate compasses. The accuracy of these two instruments was crucial to our success in navigating whatever ocean expanse we were going to be called upon to cross. No question, these instruments had to be accurately checked and, if necessary, corrected.

The magnetic compass can be and usually is calibrated (swung) on the ground. However, the flux gate compass can only be calibrated in flight. We had no trouble with the pilot's and navigator's magnetic compasses; however, there was a problem with the flux gate (also called a remote or gyro) compass.

The flux gate compass is comprised of two major components: the sensing unit located (as I recall) in the outer portion of the left wing and two compass-like indicators, one of which is mounted on the pilot's side of the instrument panel, and the other on the navigator's panel. The sensor detects the lines of magnetic force which make up the earth's magnetic field. The information so gathered is converted into an electrical signal which is relayed to the indicators. It functions as a back up to the magnetic compass. In at least two important respects, it is superior to the magnetic compass. It does not have the turning error characteristic inherent in the magnetic compass; and the finer graduations of the dial and overall stability of the indicator make it possible to establish and maintain more precise headings. In practice, the magnetic compass backs up the flux gate compass.

For some reason or other, we experienced difficulty in getting it calibrated. As a result, we put more hours on our airplane than most of the other fellows did on theirs. This extra flying time, I believe, turned out to be a blessing in disguise.

On August 4, 1944, our orders came through. The subject of the orders cleared some of the doubt. It read: "Movement Orders, Heavy Bombardment Crew Number FV-900-CJ-88, To Overseas Destination." Further down in the text was the admonition: "You will not file safe arrival telegrams with commercial agencies while en route and at domestic or overseas destination." The curtain of secrecy was being lowered. Our destination was the Port of Embarkation at Grenier Field, Manchester, New Hampshire. Since we were starting out to the east, it would be very unlikely that we were slated for the Asian Theater of Operation. Clearly, we were under strict orders not to land at any other location than Grenier Field unless an extreme emergency arose.

So, on August 7, 1944, we were directed to take off shortly after midnight. Departures from Kearney for overseas destinations were scheduled at night in order to make it difficult for enemy agents (if any were around) to accurately determine the number of airplanes leaving the base and the direction they were going.

We took off to the west. After gaining a couple of thousand feet of altitude, we turned to the east and continued to climb to our assigned altitude which, I recall, was 8,000 feet. This was to be our longest flight, up to this time, as a crew. It would be about 1,300 miles which should take approximately six and three quarter hours to fly from Kearney to Manchester.

Our flight path would take us either over or very near to Des Moines, Chicago, Toledo, Erie and Albany and on to Manchester.

Soon the lights of Des Moines passed underneath us as we continued on our way to Chicago. Nearing Chicago, we over flew a deck of low clouds and lost sight of the ground. This meant that we could no longer rely upon pilotage to confirm the accuracy of our dead reckoning navigation fixes. Earlier we had flown under an overcast which eliminated celestial navigation. Now, we had to rely solely upon radio and dead reckoning navigation. We had been in the air long enough to have established wind direction and velocity with reasonable accuracy. This, in turn gave us confidence in our dead reckoning calculations. The airplane was now a pretty laid back operation.

"Iron Mike", the autopilot, was in control and we were "flying the beam" which came through loud and clear. There was a group of three or four of the crew gathered in the cockpit with Tom and me. We were speculating about our final destination. As our point of departure was Manchester, it appeared that the deck was stacked in favor of England. Therefore, it must be England. However, there was still the possibility we could head for the Azores and the Mediterranean theatre if our route from Manchester took us to Gander, Newfoundland.

While this discussion was going on, one of the fellows happened to look down through the crawl way opening in the cockpit floor. His comments were something to this effect: "HEY!! There's something wrong with the voltage regulators!! They look like they're on fire!!" I checked the generator volt meters and all four of the needles were pegged at the high end of the scale. I immediately turned the generator switches off. This took the voltage regulators out of their self destruct mode. However, my action wasn't quick enough, as all of the radios and most of the lights went out and "Iron Mike" decided to go to sleep.

We were now in a fix. It was night, we had no radios and were caught between two cloud layers. Also, the autopilot was inoperative, although this was a minor inconvenience at this time. When the voltage regulators failed, they had allowed the voltage to rise and "fry" most of the more voltage sensitive equipment which happened to be turned on at the time. As luck would have it, all of the radios were gone. That included the command, radio compass and liaison sets. The VHF had been off but no ground stations monitored VHF frequencies. So, it was of no help.

It was decision time. I considered our situation qualified as an extreme emergency as provided for in our orders. Do we try to find a place and land? Or do we press on until it becomes daylight and hope to land at Grenier? For some reason or other, we never thought about or discussed returning to Kearney. I guess our mind set was "We're on our way and we're not turning back."

Charlie Dye, the Tail Gunner, was definitely sure our problem qualified as an "extreme emergency" —- thus it would be O.K. for us to go to and land at Cleveland. Which, by some coincidence, was close to his home. I hated to disappoint him.

101

It now remained to consider two important factors: the airplane and the weather.

The first consideration was the airplane. The airplane was flying and there was no indication or apparent danger which would keep it from continuing to do so. The batteries would probably carry what little electrical load we had left and would need to use later. When it came time to land, we could always manually lower the flaps and the gear. The engines continued to run on their magnetos and the electronic turbocharger control still worked. The airplane "said" continue to Grenier.

The second consideration included the weather and the time of day. We knew that clouds were underneath us. What we didn't know was: how much ceiling is there under those clouds? Without a radio there was no way to find out. Except, to go down there and see for ourselves. While it was early in the morning, it was still pitch dark. In my book, it is not real smart to go stooging around just above the ground, in the clouds, in the dark, while looking for an airport. An airport, about whose location, you didn't have a clue. The weather and the time of day combined to "say" continue to Grenier.

The "vote" two to zero to go for Grenier. We continued on course (we hoped) to Grenier.

From here on it would be strictly up to Columbus' dead reckoning. The clouds continued to be above us too, so, any celestial fixes were out of the question. Tom and I really paid attention to our heading and air speed. If we got lost, it would not be the result of poor piloting.

As dawn broke and it began to get light, we calculated that we should be somewhere over western New York State.

It was decision time again. Do we continue on this course and at our present altitude until we reach our estimated time of arrival at

Grenier? Or, do we go down and see if we can get under the lower level of clouds and go the rest of the way using pilotage?

It was decided it was time to take a peek. The consensus among Columbus, John, Tom and me was that we were probably pretty close to Albany, New York now. I asked Columbus to check his chart for the highest point within a 30 mile radius of Albany. I planned to spiral down from our present altitude to no lower than 500 feet above this highest point. If we broke out in the clear before that altitude was reached, that would be fine. If we didn't, it was time to spiral back up to our previous altitude and continue on our original course. Spiralling up and down would affect our position and dead reckoning calculations the least.

Columbus came back shortly with "It looks like you can go down to 2,500 feet O.K." We started down slowly, 250 feet per minute. We plunged into the clouds. Soon the clouds began to thin. Through them, occasionally, we caught glimpses of the ground; however, we couldn't see enough of the ground to confidently establish our position. The altitude was 3,000 feet. About that time, Columbus came back with "There is one peak at 2,800 feet. I missed it earlier." This really shook me. If it was nearby, I hoped the airplane would also miss it. If it wasn't near, we could drop down another couple of hundred of feet and take a look at the ground. Then we could establish our position with certainty.

From the short glimpses we caught of the ground, it looked like it was far enough below the bottom of the clouds so we could go on down the few extra feet. Obviously, we didn't hit anything. Otherwise you wouldn't be reading this.

We were almost directly over Albany. However, the clouds were sitting on top of the mountains all along the ridge of mountains to the east of the city. There was no way out of that basin to the east without getting into the clouds. Even to the south along the Hudson River, the ceiling was practically zero. Lady Luck obviously was riding with us. We "screwed" ourselves back up to our original altitude and continued on our previous course. We, at least, knew exactly where we were and could revise our dead reckoning plan position accordingly. We had to assume no change in the wind direction and velocity.

If the undercast continued, our plan was to overfly Grenier and proceed until we were reasonably sure we were out over the ocean. Once over the ocean, we could go down on the deck, 50 to 200 feet above the water, and head back toward land. We hoped that the clouds had a base and that there was not a layer of fog on top of the water.

There are mountains around Grenier; however, there is an opening in the direction of our approach from the east. If there was enough ceiling to let us maintain 1,000 feet altitude, we could make our way to Grenier. However, if the ceiling was so low as to make 1,000 feet impossible, we'd head for the nearest airport and land.

When we believed we were over the ocean we started to let down. We broke out of the clouds over the ocean at about 1,500 feet altitude. From there on "It was a piece of cake." We turned back to the west and slipped under the base of the clouds. It didn't take long to make landfall and soon we hit Grenier Field right on the nose.

After almost 7 hours of flying, we landed safely, although a bit tired, at Grenier. We would be there several days while the airplane was fixed. All of the radios needed repair. The batteries, located in the wing, had boiled over when the voltage regulators went "ape". So the batteries had to be replaced and the spilled acid washed out of the wing. I pointed out to the maintenance people that the autopilot also was inoperative. They told me they didn't have the stuff to fix it and, besides, the airplane would fly without it. So, wherever we were going, it would be up to Tom and me to hand fly the thing the whole way. That is, unless we could get the autopilot fixed somewhere along the route.

Soon, on August 12, the bird was again flyable. I requested a local flight so we could make sure that it was O.K. for the next leg, whatever that was going to be. My request was granted. When we got ready to try it out, a number of the base aircraft maintenance and other personnel were standing around the plane. They knew we were going up for a local (area) flight. Finally, one of them got up the courage to ask, "Sir, could we go along? We've never flown in a B-17." As we had only a skeleton crew aboard, I told about a half dozen of them to go get parachutes and get aboard.

We got airborne and proceeded to check out the electrical equipment. Everything, except the autopilot, worked fine. However, to make sure, it seemed only logical to take a short cross country. I also felt it was unfair to limit the B-17 experience to just those base personnel who were on board. It was a nice, warm, clear, sunny August day. A perfect day for the beach. This meant there would probably be a lot of people at the beach. An excellent opportunity for us to "Inspect the Beach" and for the Boston beach goers to see a B-17 up real close and real fast. We made several passes along the beach out over the water at about 200 feet altitude. This turned out to be one of those rare occasions where everybody wins.

We spent two and one half hours examining the area. The Base personnel really enjoyed the trip. Judging from the waving of the crowd on the beach, they, too, enjoyed it.

I figured if we were reported, the worse that would happen to us would be for the Base C.O. to deny us our trip overseas. To be deprived of that experience didn't worry me at all. We weren't reported. Or, if we were, the Base chose to ignore it.

For the first time in my brief Army career, on August 7, 1944, I was given "SECRET" orders. Up until this time, all of my orders had been classified "RESTRICTED". These orders cleared up the uncertainty of our destination. We were instructed to "… depart … via North Atlantic Route to the European Theatre of Operations … for further assignment and duty with the 8th Air Force."

I had to pinch myself as I remembered only 17 years previously, Lindbergh had been the first to fly solo across the Atlantic. Now, here I was about to do it myself. Not solo, but to fly the Atlantic.

In the years since this flight, I have never ceased to be amazed at the planning detail which had gone into making it possible for a bunch of still-wet-behind-the-ears pilots to successfully cross the ocean. We were to proceed as single ships; thus, we would be entirely on our own.

As a part of the briefing, we were shown a film which had been taken from the cockpit of a B-17. This film showed all of the approaches for the emergency fields between Grenier and our next destination, Goose Bay, Labrador. The film was shown several times. Therefore, when we actually flew the route, it felt as if we had been there several times before.

We were again on our way on the 15th of August. When we passed over the emergency fields at Presque Isle, Maine and on the north shore of the St. Lawrence River, we saw several B-17's on the ground. Later we found out that they had also suffered voltage regulator failures. The extra flying we had done at Kearney had apparently caused our voltage regulator problem to surface on the trip from Kearney to Grenier.

About five hours and some 850 miles later, we landed at Goose Bay without a hitch. Even though it was August, the days were cool and the nights cold. I asked to get the autopilot fixed. But, the story was the same as the one at Grenier. No parts. There were a couple more 17's grounded here with voltage regulator problems.

Then it was the briefing for next leg of the journey — which was to be to Iceland. This leg was also covered by a film "trip". Included were the two emergency fields on Greenland, Bluie West 1 and Bluie East 1, and our destination, Keflavik, Iceland. This latter field was located on the southwest corner of Iceland not far from the Icelandic capital, Reykjavik.

106

The emergency fields on Greenland were just that. Bluie West 1 was a one runway airport located on the west coast of Greenland at the head end of a fiord. No matter the direction of the wind, you landed to the east. The final approach was some 50 miles up the fiord. If the approach was missed, you had better pour on the coal and start praying immediately. There was a mountain directly ahead and there was not enough room between the fiord walls to make a 180. If you were incredibly lucky and cleared the mountain, it would take about half an hour to get back around for the next attempt. Because of the mountain at the end of the runway, regardless of wind direction, all take offs were down the fiord. Fortunately, because of our lack of trouble and the fuel load of 3,000+ gallons (one bomb bay tank plus the mains and the Tokyo tanks) and the good weather in Iceland, we didn't have to use these meager facilities.

We were cautioned not to rely upon our radios, particularly the radio compass, to find our way to Iceland. It seems that the Germans had been known to send out false homing signals from a surfaced submarine. In this way they could lead an airplane off course. The false signal would then be turned off and the misguided airplane, as it tried to find its location, would run out of fuel and be forced down into the ocean. Given the icy nature of the North Atlantic — not a nice situation in which to be.

Our course would take us just south of Greenland. The assigned altitude was 10,000 feet. Since mountains on Greenland are higher than that, I asked Columbus to allow at least 100 miles clearance around the southern tip of Greenland. It was not that I lacked confidence in him. After all, he did a good job in the flight from Kearney to Manchester. I just wanted to be sure.

Soon we were on our way. This was going to be the longest leg of the trip. Around 1,450 miles and a good eight and one half hours would be involved. We took off in the early morning while it was still dark. In spite of the possibility of German deception with false signals, I used the radio compass as a back up to Columbus' labors.

About half way to Iceland the sun came up. It was one of the most welcome sunrises I have ever seen. This was the first time I had ever been out of sight of land. No matter which way I looked there was nothing but water. This called for extra special surveillance of the engine instruments and the fuel tank gages.

While it would have been nice to have had the autopilot to help with the flying, we got along without it. The airplane could be trimmed up so it pretty much held level and on course with only a light touch of correction now and then. Of course, if the crew did much moving bout, this upset things. However, except for Nelson, Tom, John, Jim McCue, George and me, the crew slept most of the way. After all, there was nothing they needed to do and most of the time there certainly wasn't much to see.

After almost nine hours, we made landfall right on the button. Columbus had kept us on the straight and narrow. We landed, and as we turned off the end of the runway, a "Follow Me" jeep swung in front of us. At first, the jeep driver looked familiar. But I dismissed that as an improbability. When we reached the ramp, however, I got a better look at the driver. Sure enough, it was "Shorty" Cannon from Washington. After the engines were shut down I yelled out the window, "Hi Ya, Shorty!" This really surprised him. We chewed the fat for awhile. He gave me the low down on the island and I brought him up to date on the happenings in Washington as I last knew them. He was about to go bananas on the island. The place is a barren rock pile, and the natives were not at all enthralled with the American presence. To avoid any problems, we were asked to stay on the base.

I never have seen, before or after, so many smooth, round rocks —- from little bitty ones to huge ones as big as houses.

Again, as at other bases on our journey, a couple of B-17's were grounded due to voltage regulator failures. Still no repair parts for the autopilot.

The next stop was to be England. Destination would be Valley, Wales on the northwest corner of Wales. The alternate, in case weather closed Valley, would be Prestwick, Scotland. There were no emergency fields between our departure point and land fall on the British Isles. Once more, there were the movies —- showing the approaches to both Prestwick and Valley.

This time our takeoff was in daylight. Previous ones had been in the dark to make it difficult for anyone to count the number of planes and note the direction in which they departed. Observation of aerial activity on Iceland would almost have to be done from the sea, and daylight made it too hazardous for either a small boat or a surfaced submarine to hang around to count, identify and track airplanes.

While we were going as individual aircraft, there was a stream of aircraft at intervals of about 15 minutes. When about half way to England from Iceland, we picked up a radio transmission from another plane. It was, in a panic stricken voice, "We're on fire. Going Down." The transmission was too short to allow a radio compass fix. Nor was the transmission repeated. In the thought it might have been an airplane in front of us, we kept all eyes on the ocean for a possible sighting. We saw nothing.

Therefore, either we were not on the same track as the airplane in distress or it was behind us. Never heard anymore from or about it. Could it be another B-17 with a voltage regulator failure/fire problem?

The weather was good so we headed for Valley, Wales where we landed after a flight of about five and one half hours. The day was August 19, 1944.

We got our gear out of the airplane. Then, I started looking for someone to give me a receipt for one B-17G, serial number 43-38286. Soon, I found someone and was I ever glad to get that receipt. I had visions of losing the thing and having to fork over $300,000 plus the cost for four engines and propellers and all of the radio equipment.

On my pay of $195 per month, I would have taken a hell of a long time to settle that debt. I still have the receipt —— just in case one day somebody from the Government shows up and says, "About that B-17 you were issued in Kearney, Nebraska back in 1944..".

Tom, McCue and I were asked to go into a conference room at Headquarters. A civilian entered and introduced himself as a member of the FBI. He asked us to sit down as he had some questions he wanted to ask us. He wanted to know if we had any problem with the voltage regulators in our aircraft. We gave him the story of our experiences including the radio message we had picked up on the way to Valley. He said sabotage of the voltage regulators was suspected as there had been a number of incidents.

When our voltage regulator problem occurred, I was more than a little bit unhappy. However, now I had a different opinion, I now believed we were fortunate to have had our problem at night. During the daylight, the overheating of the regulators would likely not be seen. In that case, the excessive voltage could easily start a fire. The voltmeters would indicate such a problem, however, their location was such that they were not regularly scanned by the Pilot nor were they located so that the Copilot could easily see them. Once a fire got going in the location of the voltage regulators, it would be strictly bad news. We never heard any more about the case.

On August 22, 1944, we were put on a train and sent to the Combat Crew Replacement Depot at Bovingdon. While waiting for our assignment at Bovingdon, we attended classes to acquaint us with some of the British customs and habits. In one of the sessions, the briefing Officer gave a good example of differences between British and American views of their environment. The intent was to prepare us so we would foster good relations between the two peoples. The example he used went something like this:

> "If you had a visitor from Britain in your home
> town and you wanted to show him around, where
> would you take him? You would take him to see the

INSTRUCTIONS:
(Give Transport Pilot 3 copies and collect 2 M/R forms he has.)

War Department
A.A.F.Form No.99
Revised May 14, 1942

WAR DEPARTMENT
Army Air Forces

XDebit   XCredit

MEMORANDUM RECEIPT

No. _____

Station _56?_   Date _19 aug 1944_

Issuing _J. C. Walter 2nd Lt_

Issued to __Detachment B, Supply Section BAD No.1__

Quantity	Unit	Part No.	Article
One	Ea		Type _B17_ and contents listed on AC Form 263 and 263A

A/C Serial No. _43-38756_

Flight Order No. _FV-CJ 88_

Project No. _9780 JR_

Confidential Equipment Installed on this A/C

Radio _Yes_

Bombsight _No_

I acknowledge receipt of the above listed Army Air Forces Property:

xStrike out words not applicable.

Charles D. O'Brien
CHARLES D. O'BRIAN
Captain, AC
Commanding.

RECEIPT FOR ONE (1) EACH B-17

NEW high school, the NEW post office, the NEW
department store and anything else NEW.

On the other hand, if you were to visit him, in his
home town, he would show you the OLD Town Hall,
the OLD Cathedral, the OLD Castle and other OLD
things.

The point is DO NOT BRAG ABOUT YOUR
NEW POSSESSIONS OR THINGS AND DO
NOT DISPARAGE HIS OLD BUILDINGS AND
CUSTOMS"

For me, that was very good advice. Then, and when living in
Scotland in 1958-59.

While we were at Bovingdon, we got to know British bees. As
houseflies are uncommon in England, screens and screen door are
seldom used. Screens were almost never used on military buildings.
This meant that our meals were always served in the company of
honey bees. They had a particular liking for orange marmalade.
The open jar was usually well covered with them. Perhaps for
this reason, to this day, I have little liking for orange marmalade.
Fortunately, these were the friendliest bees I've ever encountered. I
don't remember hearing of anyone getting stung.

We also began our acquaintance with the British currency. The
only thing in common with U.S. currency was the word penny. And
the pennies were almost the size of a silver dollar!! From there on it
was a real mind boggler. Twelve pence (pennies) made up a shilling.
Only the shilling was usually called a "bob". It took 20 shillings
to make a pound. But to help "clarify" things, in addition to the
shilling coin, there was a myriad of other coins. Such as: a half
crown coin. (Only half crowns. No crowns. A half crown was equal
to two shillings and six pence. Got that clear?) Farthings (1/4th of a
penny), half pennies (hay'p nay), three pennies (thrup nay bit), six

pennies (six pence) and two shillings. And if that was not enough, one pound plus one shilling, or 21 shillings, was a Guinea.

The paper currency in common circulation was limited to a 10 shilling, one pound and five pound notes. (In U.S. currency these three bills were roughly equivalent to a $2, $5 and $20 bill, respectively.) Unlike U.S. paper money, they were all of a different size. The higher the denomination of the bill, the larger the bill. The 5 pound note was printed on one side of white paper. We called them bed sheets. They were rather scarce. In fact, at times the establishment taking the bill would ask you sign it on the back. In spite of its watermark, this bill must have been easy to counterfeit.

Most of us never got used to the coins or the bills. They seemed like Monopoly money. And, it was easy to fall into the trap of treating one pound notes as one dollar bills. At the official exchange rate of $4.035 to one pound, treating "$5 bills" like they are $1 bills could quickly and easily lead to bankruptcy.

On September 5, 1944 we were given orders to report to the 95th Bomb Group (H).

We were getting closer and closer to the shooting war.

CHAPTER 11
JOINING THE 95TH BOMB GROUP

We were one of six crews sent from Bovingdon to the 95th Bomb Group (H). The (H) stands for Heavy. On checking in at Headquarters, we were told we were being assigned to the 412th Bomb Squadron (H). The Commanding Officer was Major Pomeroy.

The 95th was located in East Anglia close by the small village of Horham. East Anglia is the bulge of England which lies northeast of London. Directly across the English Channel to the east is the Netherlands.

The base was typical of the many bases in this area. It had been hastily built shortly after the war started. In order to conserve resources, to make the field less conspicuous from the air, and less susceptible to bombing damage, little earth moving had been done. The runways had the same rolling nature as those at Dyersburg. In order to disturb things the least, a small road was not relocated but was allowed to cross the main runway. Further, the barracks and other supporting buildings were well scattered about the country side in order to make them less likely to be damaged by any German bomb coming that way.

This arrangement of facilities required more than a little getting used to. Unlike the bases in the States, there were no nice straight streets with signs to guide us from one point to another.

Instead, the various buildings were connected by meandering foot and bicycle paths. Paths which wound all around the place like so many cow paths. They were not too bad in the daytime but at night, in the blackout, they were a real challenge to follow. Particularly, after a long evening spent at the Officer's Club, partaking in a session which could impair our navigational faculties more than a little bit.

The Nissen huts for the Officers were in groups of four and shared a common, but separate, toilet facility. Usually, the Officers from two crews, eight men in all, were assigned to a single hut.

The Nissen hut, when viewed from the end, was semicircular in shape. The hut was made by fastening curved sheets of corrugated iron to the inside and outside of the steel arches which comprised the frame. Other than the air space between the inner and outer steel shells, there was no insulation between the two walls. In fact, the hut looked like it was made from half of a large corrugated steel drainage tile.

The ends were closed up with wood. Both of the ends had a door and two windows, one on either side of the door. However, the door at one end usually was nailed shut to keep out the drafts. The windows were covered with blackout curtains which were seldom opened. So, regardless of the time of day or amount of sunshine (very rare), the interior always seemed like a cave. The floor was concrete. Make that cold, cold, damp concrete. Inside was always damp and musty.

A small coke burning stove was in the center of the building. This ensured that those occupants with beds in the center of the room were usually toasted. While those with beds near the end of the building thought they were living inside a glacier.

My bunk was just inside the door on the left side. Across the aisle was George Hail's bunk. George was a rotund person who had done a stint in the RAF prior to joining the U.S.A.A.F. and the 8th. George was a quiet person who spent a lot of time reading. His crew members, however, were more than a bit on the wild side.

For a short time, there were nine of us in the hut. The extra person was a bombardier by the name of "Frank" (Francis) Pierce. His crew had finished the required number of missions and had been sent back to the States. However, Frank had missed out on a couple of missions so he had to stay until those had been completed. As I recall, he was from Cincinnati. We hit it off real well for the short time he was there.

From my bed down "my" side of the hut were Columbus, John and Tom in that order. George's crew was along "his" side of the hut. Lining the crew up along one side of the hut made it easier for the orderly to find and wake those scheduled for a mission.

Along the walls of the hut were clothes racks made from pipe. Completing the furnishings were shelves/storage spaces made from old ammunition and shipping boxes. And there was the inevitable footlocker.

The beds were almost luxurious. They were three quarter size with a decent mattress and springs. Blankets were sufficient in quantity; however, they were filthy dirty. It took a long time to get them cleaned. Furthermore, there was considerable reluctance to send the blankets out for cleaning since you might not get them back. There were no sheets, so this meant sleeping next to the blankets in your underwear.

Few had the courage to either own or wear a pair of pajamas. In a short space of time I did manage to get a pair of sheets from a homeward bound Officer. It took quite a while to get sheets washed. All of our washing was done by nearby British women. We had to provide the soap as it was in short supply for British civilians. After we had been there a couple of months, I picked up, for TWENTY TWO <u>1944</u> DOLLARS, another pair of sheets at Harrods in London. The quality was very outstanding. For the price I paid, it should have been. When I returned to the States I took those pricey sheets with me. Mother used them for years.

Original hut lighting was a string of about six 20 Watt light bulbs down the center the building. This fell far short of our needs. This situation was corrected by striping the lights and wiring out of the common toilet facility. The wiring and lights in the toilet would be replaced by base maintenance when there were enough complaints. After the hut lighting had been improved a few times, the circuit would be overloaded and all of the lights would go out. This time the base maintenance people came through the barracks and stripped out all of the jury rigged lights. The cycle would be repeated in a relatively short time. The wiring was not 110 volts but 220 so judiciousness was called for when making wiring changes without the power shut off.

We soon found the ration of coke/coal, like the hut lighting arrangement, to be woefully inadequate, even for those adjacent to the stove. It did not take long to learn that our supply of fuel could be augmented by a "midnight requisition" from the Officers' Club or other source. The thievery assignment rotated among the hut occupants. Thus, everyone became a thief. Peer pressure, if not rank, ensured no innocents.

The toilet facilities, more commonly called the latrine, were in a brick building which lacked any heat, hot water or glass in the "window" openings. Also theft of the wiring, switches and light bulb sockets made the place as dark as a cave. This obviously resulted in the latrine being used only when absolutely necessary. Lingering and reading therein just did not occur.

Near the hut was a slit trench bomb shelter. Fortunately, we never had need to use it. However, when we went outside to watch a V-1 Buzz Bomb go by, we always made sure our vantage point was near the shelter. If the Buzz Bomb engine quit while it was near us, we could make a quick dive for cover. We were somewhat off the V-1 track for London, so about the only ones we saw were those which had strayed off course. None ever landed near the Base, while we were there.

Near Headquarters, there was a communal bath house. It, too, was devoid of heat; however, sometimes there was hot water. It was equipped with both bath tubs and showers. The windows did have glass in them. And the doors were solid; however, there were substantial gaps at the top and bottom. The bath house, like the latrine, was not a place to linger. You did what you had to do and moved on.

The showers were controlled by a spring loaded valve in the shower head. To turn the shower on required a steady pull on a chain. It was an obvious and effective step to conserve water, more specifically, almost hot water. However, it is near impossible to wash with one hand and to hang onto the shower control with the other. So, this was the drill which it was necessary to follow: wet yourself; apply soap; rinse off. It worked; but it wasn't as near as enjoyable as having a continuously running shower since we damn near froze when the lukewarm water was not running.

On one of my first trips to the Officers' Club, who should I run into but Dr. Jack McKittrick. He was the son of our family Doctor in Washington. I had known him for a long time. He was a flight Surgeon with the rank of Captain, in the 95th and the 336th Squadron almost since the group had been formed in the States. Small World.

We spent a great deal of time exchanging news from home. He was particularly anxious to hear anything I knew, as he had not been home for almost two years. Dr. Jack told me Clay Embry, a fellow who had been in High School with me, also was a member of the 95th. Small World, again.

"THE HUT", HOME FOR EIGHT MONTHS.
"THE FACILITY" IS THE BUILDING AT THE LEFT

We had arrived at the 95th just in time to take part in the Group's celebration of its 200th mission. It was a real good party. Complete with Glenn Miller and his band. Sadly, Glenn was lost on a flight to France shortly after this show.

We did not have much time to settle in before we were put to work. There was the inevitable bout with the Link Trainer and Ground School. Then the equally inevitable check ride. By now, I had more than 500 hours in my log book, my instrument rating and had flown the Atlantic. Still, there was the check ride. This happened on September 22, 1944. I passed.

CHAPTER 12
FLYING COMBAT

At this point I think that it would help in the understanding of the narrative in the following chapters if I would present some information about how it was to fight a war between four and six miles above the surface. When you look upon a serene blue sky, either from the ground or from a seat in an airliner, it is difficult to imagine that what seems so benign is, in fact, an extremely dangerous space. This hostile environment comes about due to a combination of extreme cold plus an atmosphere lacking sufficient air density for man to live.

HIGH ALTITUDE AIDS DEFENSE

Our missions were usually flown above 20,000 feet. Our highest was 30,000 feet. The reason for these high altitudes was purely defensive both in respect to German fighter aircraft and anti aircraft guns.

In respect to the German fighter aircraft whose mission was to shoot us out of the sky, the higher we were, the longer it took them to get to our altitude. In addition, in the act of climbing they would have to burn more of their dwindling fuel supply just to get a chance to take a shot at us.

As to the anti aircraft fire, the higher our flight level, the shorter the time an individual gun would have us in range. The bulk of the German heavy antiaircraft guns consisted of 88 mm (about a 3-1/2" diameter shell) artillery pieces fitted to carriages or platforms that allowed them to shoot almost vertically. Before the shell was loaded into the gun, the shell fuse would be set (cut) so when the shell reached the predetermined altitude, it would explode. The resulting shrapnel was intended to bring down the enemy aircraft, us.

Early in the war ranging and tracking of the shells and guns were done through optical sights. Thus, the higher the target, the more difficult it was to see and to hit. Near the end of the war the Germans acquired radar artillery control capabilities. This improved their ability to track our course, determine our altitude and speed and set shell fuse timing. No longer did clouds provide a hiding place for our aircraft.

The range of an antiaircraft gun is a hemisphere which, for illustration purposes, may be viewed as a half of a grapefruit. Continuing this illustration, put the cut side of the grapefruit on the ground and center it on the gun position. The outside skin of the grapefruit is the range of the gun. That is, the shell shot by the gun can go no farther than the skin of the grapefruit. From this it is obvious that if we could fly high enough to not pierce the grapefruit skin we wouldn't get shot. Unfortunately, the guns could shoot higher than we could fly. However, the higher up we could go, less was the time the gunners on the ground could shoot at us.

When the anti aircraft shell, commonly called "flak", exploded it did so with a deep red flash usually followed by a dumb bell shaped greasy black cloud of smoke. If they were close to your aircraft the explosion could be heard over the roar of the engines. Even closer, you could hear the rattle of the shell fragments as they hit or pierced the aircraft's skin. If the explosion was in or very near your intended flight path it would result in a bump from the air turbulence it created. These black puffs were more than a little

THE 95TH UNDER A FLAK ATTACK

intimidating. Particularly, when following another Group into the "shooting gallery". Looking ahead, you knew you were going to get the same, or worse, treatment when you came in to range. These blankets of smoke bursts gave rise to saying: "Flak so heavy you can walk on it."

PERSONAL COMFORT AND PROTECTION

Unlike the newer B-29, the crew areas of the B-17 were not pressurized. Thus, it was necessary to use oxygen masks continuously above 10,000 feet. At the altitudes we most often flew, the temperatures were always quite cold. Usually, they ranged between 40°F and 65°F <u>BELOW ZERO</u>.

The cockpit and nose sections of the B-17 were equipped with heaters. However, I don't recall ever flying an airplane with a heater that actually worked. Because of this, it was necessary for us to dress so we could sit in that deep freeze for five or more hours and not turn into a icicle.

To prepare myself for these sessions in the "cooler", this is how I dressed. I first put on my regular olive drab boxer shorts and tee shirt. Then on top of that went two piece (shirt and drawers) long "johns", then a wool khaki Class B shirt and pants, followed by a two piece electrically heated flying suit and topped off with a gabardine flying suit and an A-2 leather jacket.

It was considered bad luck to have cleaned a "lucky" uniform. A "lucky" uniform" being one you had on when you returned unscathed from the latest mission. Therefore, I wore the same khaki Class B's for the entire 35 missions without benefit of cleaning. By the 35th mission, the salt rings under the arm pits were rather crusty and certainly of monumental size. (Even though it was unbelievably cold, more than once situations arose which caused me to sweat, profusely.) The inside of the shirt collar also had a nice layer of grease. When I finished, it was cleaned and is now in my closet.

For the feet it was two pairs of socks, G.I. high top shoes, JCW modified electrically heated boots and fleece lined flying boots. The hands were covered by silk gloves and topped with electrically heated fleece lined leather gloves. The purpose of the silk gloves was to prevent your fingers sticking to any very cold metal surfaces should it be necessary to remove the bulky heated gloves to perform an adjustment not possible while wearing the heated gloves.

By each crew member station there was an electrical outlet with a rheostat control knob. The upper portion of the heated suit had a cord with a plug on the end of it. Just like a toaster. The lower portion of the suit connected electrically to the upper part with snap connections somewhat similar to 9V battery connectors. Connections for the gloves and the boots were provided at the end of the suit sleeves and legs, respectively. When all these connections had been made we were really wired.

To explain the JCW modified heated boots. The regular issue of heated boots were thin felt slipper-like things to which the heating wires were stitched. These worn directly over your socks. The fleece lined flying boots were worn over these electrically heated slippers. This system did not appeal to me. I had heard if you bailed out with this arrangement, the shock of the parachute opening could result in yanking you right out of the fleece lined and the electrically heated boots. In which case, when you landed you would be in your stocking feet. Not a real good state of affairs to either begin a hike in enemy territory or take up residency in a German POW camp. To get around this little problem, I cut the wires off of the felt boots, wrapped the wires around my G.I. high tops and put the fleece lined boots over them. I always had toasty feet, and no worry about having to plod around in Germany or any where else in my stocking feet.

Speaking about walking around in Germany, one of the pieces of equipment we carried on each mission was an escape kit. This was a packet which included a map of Europe (printed on silk cloth), some German occupation currency, a compass and a couple of personal photos. Film was scarce in the occupied areas which made it

ESCAPE KIT PHOTOGRAPHS

**IN THE EVENT OF EITHER BEING SHOT OR FORCED
DOWN IN ENEMY HELD TERRITORY, THESE PHOTOS
COULD BE USED BY THE UNDERGROUND RESISTANCE
TO MAKE FORGED IDENTITY DOCUMENTS**

difficult to get photos for fake identity papers. Thus, we were provided with photos. Where did I get that handsome sport coat? The Group photographer had coats in a range of sizes which were used for the picture taking session. Since the photographer's selection of haberdashery was limited, there was the very distinct possibility of the Germans finding a number of "dress-a-likes" running around in the Fatherland.

Protection for face and head was provided by the oxygen mask, headset, sun glasses and flak helmet or Officer's cap. The latter was worn only when not being shot at. While being shot at — the steel helmet.

As time at altitude accumulated, moisture from the breath would condense and leak out around the bottom of the oxygen mask. As this condensation dripped down the front of my jacket it would freeze. So, after a while, a big icicle would form on the front of my jacket. Moisture from my hands would gradually work its way through the gloves and, in time, the back of the gloves would have a nice coating of frost on them.

Of course, on top of the A-2 jacket was the parachute harness and, just in case we were unfortunate enough to land in the Channel or the North Sea, the Mae West (life jacket) provided the top layer. When we were over enemy territory, the flak jacket (vest) became the icing on the cake.

The flak vest, a forerunner of today's bullet proof jacket worn by the police, was made up of approximately 1-1/2 inches wide horizontal strips of steel sown into an apron-like canvas garment. The strips overlapped like shingles, giving a degree of flexibility without compromising protection. The vest was held in place by neck and waist straps. The lower edge of the front of the vest dipped down in the center far enough to offer protection to certain vital personal equipment. Some air crew members used extra flak vests to armor the bottom of the seats (again, to protect certain vital equipment) and other adjacent surfaces. Charlie, our tail gunner, was a master at scrounging and using extra flak vests. Due to that, our airplane was always tail heavy.

Regular issue parachutes consisted of a harness with a separate parachute pack which clipped onto the front of the harness. The pack could not be worn while the pilot was seated at the controls as it interfered with control column movement. Thus, the pack was supposed to be stored on the floor or somewhere near at hand. This did not appeal to me. I had visions of me being blown out of the airplane and finding myself at 20,000 or so feet without a parachute. I requested and was issued a back pack chute which I could wear at all times. Thus, if I did happen to get blown out of the airplane and was able to pull the rip cord, I could figure to hit the ground at a speed slow enough to make survival at least a reasonable expectation.

B-17's were not equipped with a lavatory. After some six or seven hours in the air, it was not unusual to find it necessary to answer the call of nature. In anticipation of this need, the designers of the airplane had provided a "relief tube" in the bomb bay. This was a piece of rubber tube one end of which went through the aircraft skin to the outside and on the other (the business) end there was affixed a funnel. However, few of us wished to unhook our heated suit, oxygen and headset connections and connect up a walk-around oxygen bottle to struggle to the bomb bay. As an added disincentive to use this equipment, the tube discharged in a location which ensured that the ball turret would either be "washed" or iced encrusted. A situation which did not please our ball turret gunner, Jack. The solution: one gallon hydraulic oil can with the top cut off. Spillage was not a problem as the contents froze quickly. Further, it could be used without leaving your seat. That was convenience!! It was even better than the barracks!! There we had to go outside to the latrine.

Of course, there were times when the urge could not be satisfied with the hydraulic can. This didn't happen too often. However, I do know of one case. It involved a Pilot, name Sutkowski, who lived across the path from us. He earned the very dubious distinction of flying across his first target squatting in the aisle between the pilot

**1ST LIEUTENANT RICHARD SUTOWSKI
412TH SQUADRON PILOT**

and copilot seats using his flak helmet for a purpose I'm sure the helmet designer had not foreseen. I heard later, when he got out of the service, he changed his name to Stanley. Was this an attempt to disassociate himself from this happening?

One hundred octane gas not only fueled the airplanes, it also was used for dry cleaning our uniforms and as cigarette lighter fuel.

After my uniform had been cleaned, it took about a week for the odor to leave. Or, maybe it just took that long for me to get used to the smell.

Using 100 octane gas for the cigarette lighter had its peculiar problems. When not flying, I usually carried my Zippo in the watch pocket of my uniform trousers. This, by itself, was no problem. No problem, that is, until I put a recently filled lighter in that little pocket and forgot to remove it before going flying. As the airplane climbed towards 20,000 plus feet, the change in altitude caused the gasoline to leak out of the lighter case. The gasoline would seep through the trousers, the long johns, the shorts and ultimately hit the skin. Then, it was like someone had built a fire on my stomach. With the parachute harness, the Mae West, the A-2 jacket, the gabardine flight suit and the heated suit on top of the offending piece of hardware, it took some time to get to the problem and get it corrected. The result was usually a nice, red, raw patch of skin on the lower abdomen. Not necessarily being a slow learner, after this occurred a few times, I was sure to put the lighter in an A-2 jacket pocket.

FORMATION ASSEMBLY AND FLYING

Assembling a bomber strike force was no small undertaking. In order to carry out daylight bombing with a minimal losses, it was necessary to keep the aircraft in each formation as compact as safety would allow. Also, keeping the bomber groups close together greatly enhanced the defensive strength provided by the twelve 50 caliber machine guns in each B-17.

The German fighter pilots must have had second thoughts as they bored into a formation of B-17's and saw all the red "winking eyes" of the 50's firing at him.

Also, if the bomber formations were closely knit, it was easier for our fighters to provide the needed cover.

The formation used while we were at the 95th is diagrammed on page 131. The basic building block of the formation was the three aircraft Flight or Element. The next higher order was the Squadron which consisted of four Flights for a total of 12 aircraft. By combining three Squadrons a Group was formed, a total of 36 airplanes. The number of aircraft, personnel required for both flight crews and support and the space to accommodate both of them resulted in the Group being the limiting size for a single air base. The combination of three Groups formed the next organizational unit, the Wing. The Wing was, nominally, a strike force of 108 aircraft.

On the occasions when a maximum effort was called for, the individual elements would be expanded to four aircraft by adding a plane in the "slot", the location behind and below the element lead aircraft. It was not at all unusual to even add another element to the low element and to the high element. When this was done, the size of a Group or Wing could be increased significantly.

For Group takeoff, the three Squadron lead aircraft took off first as they were the nucleus for pulling the formation together once assembly altitude was reached. After the leaders had taken off, the High, Lead and Low Squadrons followed in that order.

For straight line flight or gradual (less than 1/4th needle width) turns, the formation flew as shown.

However, when a sharper turn was required a problem would arise. To explain: assume a sharp turn to the right.

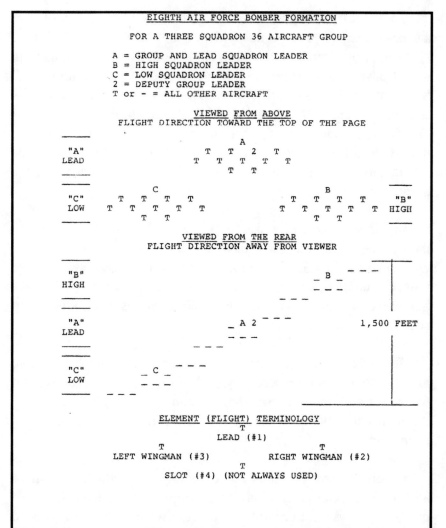

EIGHTH AIR FORCE BOMBER FORMATION

FOR A THREE SQUADRON 36 AIRCRAFT GROUP

A = GROUP AND LEAD SQUADRON LEADER
B = HIGH SQUADRON LEADER
C = LOW SQUADRON LEADER
2 = DEPUTY GROUP LEADER
T or - = ALL OTHER AIRCRAFT

VIEWED FROM ABOVE
FLIGHT DIRECTION TOWARD THE TOP OF THE PAGE

ELEMENT (FLIGHT) TERMINOLOGY

VIEWED FROM THE REAR
FLIGHT DIRECTION AWAY FROM VIEWER

The "B" High Squadron, being on the inside of the turn, will have a shorter distance to cover than will "A" or "C" Squadrons. Thus, if "B" High Squadron maintains its position relative to "A" Squadron, it will have to slow down in order to avoid getting ahead of "A" Squadron. If "B" slows sufficiently to keep its place in formation, its aircraft can approach or reach stalling speed. On the other hand, if "B" does not reduce speed, it will fly over "A". When that happens, the "B" lead pilot can very easily lose sight of "A" Squadron since it is underneath him. This is very hazardous as it frequently results in mid air collisions.

In this same case of a turn to the right, "C" Squadron, being on the outside of the turn, will have a greater distance to cover than will "A" Squadron. If "C" Squadron had sufficient available reserve power it could speed up and maintain the relationship with "A" Squadron. However, in reality, the aircraft had insufficient power to accomplish this.

To solve this turning problem, "B" and "C" Squadrons move to the left and right, respectively, and fall into trail behind "A" and follow him around the turn. Upon resuming a straight line course, the high and low squadrons "slide" back into the original spread formation.

Given the desire (necessity) of being at 20,000 feet or more altitude over Germany plus the climbing rate and air speed of the B-17, it was not possible, in most cases, to take off and head directly for the Continent climbing en route. This procedure just would not gain enough altitude before reaching enemy territory. The solution was to gain approximately one half of the desired altitude over England before heading toward the Continent. The time spent climbing also gave an opportunity to form up the Squadrons, Groups and Wings before leaving the shores of England.

The planes in each bomber group took off at 20 second intervals and headed for the assigned altitude and rendezvous point. Once the group was formed, it headed to another rendezvous point. There, it met with the other groups (usually 2) to form the three Group Combat Wing. In turn, the Combat Wing would head for the coastal departure point and fall into its assigned position in the attacking bomber stream.

If the Group or Combat Wing reached the rendezvous point early, it could "burn up" the extra time by either a series of "S" turns or one more complete 360° turns. However, if they were late, a big problem was created. (On one occasion our Group got caught in this situation. More about that later.) The cruise and climb speed of the bomber stream was such that there was little extra power available to use for "catch up". Also, pulling extra power significantly increased fuel consumption which could lead to a big problem later on. This was true particularly if bad weather moved in and closed the home base, forcing either an over-the-field holding pattern or a diversion to another field.

The Group rendezvous was usually at or above 10,000 feet. For most Groups, in order to reach this altitude, the individual aircraft would depart its base on a specified heading and fly that heading at a 250 feet per minute climb rate at 135 mph air speed for a predetermined time (usually 5 minutes). At the end of the five minutes, it would make a 180° turn and, maintaining the 250 fpm climb and 135 mph air speed, fly on the new heading for the same amount of time flown on the first leg. Thus, through a series of "switch back" like maneuvers, each aircraft would work its way up to the rendezvous altitude.

Religious attention to rate of climb, speed and heading minimized the chance of mid air collisions. However, collisions did occur. When they did, particularly in the dark, the sky would be lit by a tremendous flash as six thousand gallons of gasoline and seven tons of bombs went off. Survival by anyone was improbable.

The location of the 95th was such that there was no clear straight out and straight back route from the base which could be used for assembly. Any direction would bring them close to another Group's assembly route. Because of this, our method of Group assembly was to fly in a climbing spiral pattern, with the center of the turn being the base. So, we would take off and put the airplane into a half needle width left turn and set things up for 250 fpm climb and 135 mph airspeed. Then, it was just a case of sitting back and waiting to reach the assembly altitude. At times, we were tempted to let "Iron Mike", the autopilot handle things; however, the possibility of having to take evasive action squelched that thought. "Iron Mike" was almost impossible to over power; so the time lost to turn the autopilot off could cause you to use up more time than you might have available to avoid a mid air collision.

While we were climbing through the clouds during assembly, the most nerve shattering experience was to run into someone's prop wash (air turbulence created by the propellers of an airplane). You wondered how far you were from being part of a nice, big, bright flash in the dimly lit early morning sky.

On one mission, I forget which one, we went into the clouds at around 800 feet and did not break out on top until 23,000 feet. That seemed like an eternity. About an hour and three quarters of "screwing" upwards through a blanket of clouds stuffed full of airplanes. For over 100 long minutes we sat there wondering where the other 35 airplanes of the Group were.

To those who have never done it, formation flying is easier than it may appear.

To form up the Squadron, once at assembly altitude, the lead aircraft would begin a very gradual turn to the left. For identification, they would periodically fire a predetermined flare type and color: for example, a flare which had two color flare "balls" in it. These two balls might be of the same or different color, such as a "green-green" or a "red-green". In the top of the B-17 cockpit, behind the copilot's seat, there was a fitting into which the muzzle of the flare pistol could be locked. Each aircraft carried a flare pistol and a selection of flares.

("Red-red", when used in the landing pattern, was to let emergency crews on the ground know there were wounded on board.)

As the Squadron lead flew in a big circle, the wing men would form on their particular element lead and the elements would begin to form on the Squadron lead. In this fashion, each individual aircraft was searching for only one other aircraft. To conserve fuel, all aircraft flew at the same air speed as much as possible. Thus, in order to overtake the lead and get into formation, it was necessary to turn inside the lead aircraft. In other words, "Cut 'em off at the pass." To do this, you maneuvered the airplane so the image of the lead aircraft was "frozen" at a particular location on the windshield. Hold your airplane in the attitude necessary to maintain that relationship and the lead airplane image will gradually get bigger. Before you know it, you're in position. Since your airspeed is almost the same as the lead, it is easy to slide in the proper spot without having to "yank things off" to keep from over running. (Incidentally, while we may not be conscious of it, we use this same technique when we decide whether to move over or not as another automobile enters the interstate when we go through an interchange.)

Contrary to what might be thought, the closer your plane is to the lead ship, the easier it is to fly formation. The reason is that you detect a change in speed or heading of the lead plane sooner and can use small, instead of large, corrections to keep your plane in position. Regardless of whether you fly loose or close formation, it is a lot of hard work.

The biggest problem in flying formation occurs when the lead ship either slows suddenly or makes a sharp turn toward the side on which you are flying. This means you have to reduce your speed quickly and to a lower value than the lead. Of course, airplanes don't have brakes as such. For normal formation flying we used the turbocharger control to vary the power settings and aircraft speed in small increments. The turbocharger control was a knob about 2 inches in diameter mounted to the left side of the center console. With your hand on this knob, it was simple to dial in small changes in power settings. The one knob controlled all four engines. However, if the situation called for a large power increase, it would be necessary to change propeller speed setting first to keep from over boosting the engines.

The propellers could be used as brakes. Moving the propeller control to the low pitch (high rpm) position, without a throttle or boost change, would cause the propeller to act as a brake. However, this had the inherent problem of causing a condition known as a run-away prop.

The pitch change mechanism of the propeller was operated by the use of engine oil. After flying at or near a constant rpm setting for a period of time in the cold air of high altitude without any significant change in engine speed, the reduced oil circulation in the prop hub would result in the oil becoming very thick. If a sudden and large change in power was made, the thick oil slowed the pitch change causing over speeding of the engine. Engine over speeding could result in very severe damage to either the engine and/or the propeller. Because of this, we seldom used the props as a means to slow the airplane in flight at altitude.

While not intended for such use, the engine cowl flaps made a very useful brake. In normal flight the cowl flaps were usually fully closed. So, if you needed some quick deceleration, the copilot, who was the closest to the controls, could open some or all of the four sets of cowl flaps. The advantages in using them were: they responded quickly and they did not have an appreciable effect upon the aircraft's trim. Landing flaps and the landing gear could also be used as brakes. However, their response was fairly slow — lowering either of them had a very appreciable effect on the aircraft's attitude and required resetting of the elevator trim.

Formation flying called for the pilot handling the controls to concentrate solely upon his lead aircraft. The pilot not at the controls carried the responsibility for watching the instruments and the air space around the aircraft and handling radio and intercom traffic.

The Pilot and Copilot more or less equally shared the formation flying duties. While not formally established, formation flying stints usually lasted about thirty minutes or less.

The 95th was well known for its tight formations. More than once, the 95th was left untouched while the 109's and 190's hit either the group ahead or behind us. A tight formation was very good insurance and, really, not all that hard to do.

ARMAMENT

We dropped a variety of bombs. They were of three types: General Purpose, Fragmentation and Incendiary. The General Purpose bombs came in a number of different weights from 100 pounds to 2,000 pounds. We dropped 100, 250, 500, 1,000 and 2,000 pound GP bombs. The hundred pounders were usually used against airfields for the purpose of putting (big) pot holes in the runways. The 250's and 500's were usually used for bridges and railroads. The one and two thousand pounders were principally used on city buildings and structures. We did not drop many Fragmentation bombs. When we did, it was the 260 pound size against troop concentrations. The 500 pound Incendiary bomb contained a number of small bomblets. The bomb casing would open up shortly after being dropped and cause the bomblets to scatter over a wide area. The five hundred pound Incendiary bombs were dropped, usually in combination with GP bombs, on cities —- the theory being either knock the city down or burn it up or both.

The bombs were fused, usually both in the nose and in the tail, with a fuse about 1 1/2 inches in diameter by 6 inches long having a small metal propeller on the external end. The fuse screwed into the bomb casing. Usually, the fuses were installed just before or just after the bombs were loaded into the bomb bay.

The hub of the fuse propeller carried a small arm which had a hole through it. This hole lined up with a hole in the front of the fuse casing. A cotter pin with an attached tag was placed through these holes to keep the propeller from turning. When the bombs were placed in the aircraft's bomb racks, the tags were removed and replaced with a wire, called the arming wire. One end of the arming wire was fastened to the aircraft. Thus, when the bombs were dropped, the wire would automatically be pulled out of the aligned holes in the fuse. The propeller was now free to turn as the bomb fell. After a predetermined number of revolutions of the propeller, the firing pin in the fuse was unlocked and the bomb was armed and ready to explode on contact.

In case there was a mechanical failure or any other reason for an aircraft to abort the mission, the bombs often were jettisoned in the English Channel. Before dropping the bombs, the Bombardier made sure the arming wires were removed and the fuse safely pins reinstalled. Supposedly, the bombs would drop "safe"; that is, they weren't supposed to explode. Sometimes, however, they weren't "safe". As the front lines advanced on the Continent, bomb jettison areas were established in France.

If the bomb load contained delayed action bombs, it was mandatory they be dropped in the Channel. This, for the simple reason that delayed action bombs could not be defused. Try to unscrew the fuse and the thing would go off.

BEFORE FLYING COMBAT

I doubt that anyone kept records on the amount of 100 Octane gas that was used in preflighting engines. If records had been kept, I wouldn't be surprised if these records would show that fully one fourth of the fuel used by the 8th Air Force was spent in preflighting engines.

Soon after the Group was alerted for a mission it would begin. At first, you could hear one or two engines start up, then slowly accelerate to 1000 rpm for a five to ten minute warm up period. Once the engines were warmed up, the magneto, propeller and full power checks would follow. This was repeated for each of the approximately 160 engines potentially involved for the next day's mission. Of course, if anything failed to check out, the procedure was repeated until everything was all right. Usually, the ruckus started around 11:00 P.M. and lasted well into the early morning.

This chorus of Wright Cyclone R-1820's didn't make falling asleep any easier for the combat crews. It was more a portent of bad things to come rather than a lullaby.

Shortly after we had gotten to the 95th, Tom and I had each bought a bicycle from a couple of fellows headed back to the States. We paid 8 pounds ($32 in "real" money). With these wheels it was easier for us to get about and expand our horizons.

Like all British bikes they didn't have a coaster brake. As we had all grown up using coaster brakes, it took a bit of practice to get used to the hand controlled brakes. Many times, we would want to stop and, as a matter of habit, try to apply the non-existent coaster brake. The result would be furious back pedaling before we remembered to use the hand brakes. There were two brake levers located on the handlebars under the hand grips. One lever controlled the front wheel brakes; the other the rear wheel brakes. The actual braking was accomplished by calipers which pressed brake blocks against the wheel rim. Once we got used to the fact there was no coaster brake, our biggest problem was to remember to take it easy with the front wheel brake. There was very great potential for a header over the handle bars with an overzealous application of the front wheel brake.

Shortly after we got the bikes, we were showing the other crew members the great advantage of this mode of transportation.

To verify this claim, Hasselback climbed on the handlebars of Tom's bike and asked Tom to give him a quick spin around the area. George sat on the handle bars and, to steady himself, grasped them near the brake levers. Unfortunately, George's right hand was between the brake lever and the handle bars. As the ride came to

**BACK ROW, L. TO R.: JIM PURDY, WG CHARLIE DYE,
TG JACK SHEETS, BT
JOHN WALTER, P
FRONT ROW, L TO R: NELSON KURZ, N LARRY
FRANCESCHINA, WG JIM McCUE, TT
GEORGE HASSELBACK, RO JOHN INGLEMAN, B**

an end, Tom started to apply the brake. When he did, it pinched George's ring finger. George let out a yell. This caused Tom to really clamp down on the brake. Result: George finished the ride with a broken finger (compound fracture of the end bone) which promptly grounded him.

When we arrived in England, we were a ten man crew. Now, due to diminishing Luftwaffe fighter attacks, the somewhat ineffective radio room hatch gun was removed. With that change, the Radio Operator could now man one of the waist guns and a Waist Gunner could be removed from the crew. Since Jim Purdy was both the Assistant Flight Engineer and Waist Gunner, he was the one taken off. His Mechanics' talents could be used elsewhere. So, now we were a nine man combat crew.

CHAPTER 13
THE FIRST MISSION

On the evening of September 27, 1944 we were placed on alert for the mission to be flown the next day, Thursday, September 28, 1944.

About 4:30 A.M., when the Squadron Orderly woke us and told us to be at Combat Mess by five, the response was a chorus of groans.

This would be our first mission. The usual practice was to assign members of a new crew as replacements or additions to positions with experienced crews. This would give new crew members a better sense of what combat was all about. We, however, were to be the exception and fly as a crew. We did have one experienced man aboard. Pat Murphy, starting his second tour, filled in for Hasselback, who was still grounded with a broken finger.

With chattering teeth we struggled into our clothes. I'm not sure whether the chattering teeth were due to the cold dampness of the hut, the early hour, or a deep feeling of apprehension about the unknown that lay ahead. It was probably about a 30-70 split with the temperature being the lesser influence. A quick dash to the latrine for a splash of cold water on the face, a shave and a quick brushing of the teeth was next. Given our youth, a daily shave was not always necessary. However, a smooth face made six or more hours of wearing an oxygen mask a bit more bearable.

We picked our way through the darkness to the Combat Mess. There awaited bacon, eggs, pancakes, hot coffee, toast and juice. It was a rather quiet group. Conversation was minimal and mostly one on one. No one seemed to have much of an appetite. This in spite of the fact it could be at least 10 or more hours before the next meal, if there was any next meal.

From the mess hall, it was to the briefing room, a large Nissen hut with chairs arranged theatre style. At one end of the room was a low raised stage and on the wall behind it a curtain covered map. Slowly the room filled as the crews entered the room and sat down. Where possible, the crews sat together. As in the Mess Hall, there was little conversation. What there was, was subdued. Soon, the C.O. entered the back of the room. Someone yelled, "Attention", which triggered an already tense group to quickly get to their feet and freeze at attention while the C.O. walked the length of the building and stepped upon the stage and gave the command, "At ease. Take your seats".

The C.O. introduced the Operations Officer. He then gave a short speech as to the importance of the day's mission. That done, the curtain covering the map was pulled back. As the map was exposed, a great groan arose from the experienced crews. They were all too familiar with this target's reputation. Today's target was MERSEBURG!! Merseburg was a very heavily defended synthetic oil refinery located on the Eastern border of Germany near Dresden. Today it was going to be a long trip, a long trip all the way across Germany.

Our route to the target and back was marked on the map with colored string. It was not a straight line course from our base to Merseburg and back. The route consisted of a number of different headings, none of which was very long. The purpose of this was twofold. One, to make it as difficult as possible for the Germans to deduce where we intended to strike: the other, to avoid, as much as possible, the heavier concentrations of anti aircraft guns.

When we had entered the briefing room, the Pilot of each crew had been given a mission information sheet. This was a legal sized single sheet of paper printed on both sides and absolutely chocked full of information —- such as, where each plane fit in the formation and important times such as, engine start, taxi and take off. I noticed that it did not, however, have a date on it nor did it name the target.

As the briefing ended, it was time for the "time hack". G.I. wrist watches had a feature which permitted the independent stopping, setting and restarting of the second hand. With this capability, once set, the watches of everyone on the mission would show the same time, to the second.

The briefing was completed by presentations from the Intelligence and Weather Officers.

It was now time to draw our parachutes, heated flight suits, flak vests and helmets and other combat gear.

That done, we were loaded into the back of a truck and driven out to the airplane. The enlisted crew had preceded the Officers, in order to install their guns and load the ammunition. The Officers rode out together, three or four crews per truckload. Transportation was, unlike that frequently seen in the movies, not on an over loaded jeep, but in the back of 6 X 6 Army truck.

As each plane was reached, the truck stopped and the assigned crew got out.

We reached our airplane. Columbus got on board and laid out his charts and other equipment. Ingleman ducked around the open bomb bay doors and checked the bomb loading. Columbus's and John's guns had been installed earlier by the enlisted men of our crew. Tom, McCue and I were met by the Ground Crew Chief.

He filled us in on the idiosyncrasies and/or uncorrected problems possessed by "his" airplane, U.S.A.A.F. serial number 42-97376. He accompanied the three of us as we made the preflight inspection. Satisfied, Tom, McCue and I swung up through the forward hatch and pulled it shut and latched it.

Daylight was beginning to show in the East. As we settled into our seats and pulled our seat belts tight, it was time to check the rest of the crew. Through the intercom each position was called to make sure the intercom worked and everybody was on board. Then, Tom and I went through the checklist up to the point: "engine start". We had now to sit and wait until our watches indicated it was time to start engines.

The second hand on my watch passed 12. I pointed the index finger of my right hand toward the instrument panel in front of Tom. He pushed the number one engine starter switch to the "energize" position. Slowly, the whine of the starter became louder as the inertia wheel gained speed. A few seconds later, I signaled Tom with a clenched fist, and he moved the starter switch to the "engage" position. The prop on number one engine started to turn and after several revolutions, I moved the number one engine magneto switch to the "on both" position. First, a single cylinder fired then as the other cylinders joined in the chorus of power, the prop speed increased in little jumps and white smoke began to billow from under the engine nacelle. The engine speed accelerated, the firing smoothed out and the white smoke disappeared. With a little imagination you could feel that that collection of metal pieces out there on the wing sensed that something big was in store and it was ready to give the best it could. With the gentle vibration of number one engine, the whole airplane slowly stirred to life.

The starting procedure was repeated three more times. Now, all four engines were running. The engine and the flight instruments were now alive confirming the activity of the engines and signaling the aircraft's readiness for flight. The soft vibration and drumming of the fuselage made it seem as if the aircraft was quivering in eager anticipation of the upcoming flight.

The Ground Crew was signaled to pull the wheel chocks. In the dim light of dawn, they saluted and gave us the thumbs up sign.

We were off to War.

Brakes were released and the outboard engine throttles opened slightly to start movement toward our position in the takeoff line. We moved out of the hard stand, paused at the taxiway entrance and, at the proper time, moved into the stream of airplanes.

Nose to tail, like a string of circus elephants, 36 bombers, some bright and shiny new and others in dull camouflage paint, purposefully proceeded along the taxi way.

Through the open cockpit windows came the very distinctive and almost intoxicating smell of burnt 100 octane aviation gas. The rumbling of 144 big round engines, with the potential of almost two hundred thousand horses, was punctuated with the squeal of brakes. Gentle application of the brakes served to hold the thrust of the engines in check and to maneuver the aircraft along the winding course of the taxi ways. Each brake application brought forth a squeal as brake blocks rubbed the brake drums.

Then it was time to run up and check the engines. Cockpit windows now closed to shut out the roar as each engine is checked to see if it performs as required.

Everything checks O.K.

The take off flare streaked upward from the control tower and lazily floated down. It was time to go.

Soon came our turn to move onto the runway behind the lead aircraft of our element. With partial power applied, the lead airplane brakes were released and it started the takeoff roll. For a few moments we were buffeted by the air hurtled back from the lead aircraft propellers. Our turn. We inched forward; waited the required 20 second interval; slowly advanced the throttles; released the brakes and began our roll down the runway.

After a short roll, the throttles were full open. Tom began to call off the airspeed as we seemed to move ever so slowly down the runway. This was the first time we had flown the airplane with a full load of fuel, ammunition and bombs. We had less than one mile to get 60,000 plus pounds of airplane, people, fuel and bombs up to flying speed.

As the airspeed increased the rudder became effective making it easier to keep the airplane going straight down the center of the runway.

One third of the runway now lay behind. It was time to see if the tail could be brought up a little bit. Not yet.

Half way down the runway. She still hadn't made up her mind to fly.

Finally, with two thirds of the runway gone, Tom called out "120". A little back pressure on the control column. The bouncing caused by the unevenness of the runway ceased. We were flying, just as the end of the runway flashed by only a scant few feet below. A light touch on the brakes stopped the rotation and vibration of the main landing gear wheels. A thumbs up signal to Tom and the gear started up. Then the flaps were slowly raised. Our air speed crept up to 135. The throttles and prop settings were cut back to climb power as we started our ascent to assembly altitude.

What a sight! Hundreds of airplanes appeared to be milling about aimlessly in the early morning sky. Soon, out of this seeming chaos, orderly groups of aircraft began to form. Then, if by magic, the smaller groups merged into larger groups and the larger groups fell into trail and headed toward the rising sun.

Our Group was a part of this, and we fell into our assigned position in the bomber stream. As we headed east toward the Continent, we continued in a gentle climb. A climb rate intended to get us to our penetration altitude before we reached the first line of antiaircraft guns.

About midway across the Channel panic struck us. Something was wrong!! We were less than 1/4th of the way through the mission and we had used almost 1/2 of our fuel!! A quick check showed fuel mixtures and cowl flaps were set properly and cylinder head temperatures were on the money. After a little discussion, Tom and I concluded that this situation was normal. It just took a lot of fuel to lift 60,000 pounds of airplane, people, bombs, ammunition and fuel 25,000 feet into the air.

Soon, we crossed the Dutch coast and entered enemy territory. It was time to tuck up the formation to discourage the enemy fighters. And to hope they would leave us alone and go scouting for easier pickings.

There were a few flak bursts every now and then. But nothing close. It looked just as menacing as we had been told it was.

Below us, some five miles, lay the enemy territory. However, it didn't appear threatening. In fact, it looked much the same as the friendly landscape of England.

The bomber stream wove its way across the sky tracing the path which had been diagrammed on the briefing room map.

So far, the mission had been uneventful. Soon, we would be at the target. The I.P. (initial point) was just ahead. At that time, the Group formation would change from its defensive to its bombing configuration. From this point on it would be straight and level flying

147

to the bomb release point. No evasive action would be permitted for the next 20 minutes. For the antiaircraft gunners below, we were just like ducks moving across the target area in a carnival shooting gallery.

The flak from the target defenders began. A few bursts at first. A blink of dark red light followed by a vertical dumb bell shaped cloud of greasy black smoke. Then, the bursts became more numerous. The often made comment, "Flak so thick you could walk on it," was no longer a saying. It was reality!!! The nearer we came to the target, the more intense the barrage became.

Now, it was much closer. It could be heard above the sound of the engines. Near bursts bounced the aircraft about. Shrapnel rattled off the airplane like hail stones.

Then suddenly there was a very close burst. Just ahead of us. A little bit to the right. Slightly above our altitude. Pieces of shrapnel came through the windows in the top of the cockpit. One of them hit Tom on the left side just above the flak suit and above his collar bone. He straightened up briefly then slumped over.

I called McCue in the top turret to check Tom and help him. Mac came down out of the turret, looked at Tom and sat down on the base of the turret and stayed there as rigid as a stone statue. I leaned out of the seat and banged him on the head with the palm of my right hand thinking this might shake him out of his shock and into action.

Instead, he just lowered his head and stayed put. I asked other crew members to help. Pat Murphy came forward from the radio room and, with the help from Columbus, got Tom out of the seat and down into the nose to see what could be done to help him.

During the time I was trying to get help for Tom, I had noticed number one engine must have taken a hit somewhere in the oil system as it was rapidly losing oil pressure. It was necessary to get it feathered before all the oil was lost. If all the oil were lost it would no longer be possible to stop the windmilling of the propeller. A windmilling propeller not only caused higher fuel consumption, but could also seize the reduction gearing and cause the propeller to twist off, endangering the whole aircraft. I was in time; there was enough oil left. The prop came to a stop.

The situation in the cockpit was now straightened out a bit. It was time for me to see where the rest of the formation was. Big surprise!! The only airplane in sight was another B-17 from the Group three or four hundred yards off our right wing. He, too, was in difficult straits. He had taken a flak burst just behind the tail gunner's turret. The burst had jammed the rudder forward into the vertical stabilizer and shredded all of the fabric from the elevators. Thus, he had no rudder to turn the aircraft and no elevator control to climb or dive. He was on a heading south in the direction towards Romania.

The formation was no where in sight. We were now all by ourselves deep in Germany with a wounded Copilot and one engine out. I asked Columbus for a direct course home. I saw no purpose in trying to follow the zig zag course of the group. We needed to get back as soon as possible to get help for Tom and reduce our exposure to further enemy action.

The next decision to be made was whether to call for friendly fighter escort or not. This was an option open to us. In the mission information sheet distributed in the briefing there were the codes to be used in just such a case as ours. However, in Officers' Club conversations it had been said the Germans listened to this frequency and, more often than not, beat the "Little Friends" to the bomber in distress. Taking our position deep in enemy territory into consideration, I figured there was a very high probability the enemy would be the first to answer our call. So, I opted not to call for help.

Columbus gave me the course for the base. I figured our best bet was to get out of enemy territory as fast as possible. Thus, it would be a good idea to trade our altitude for speed. Altitude was a defense against antiaircraft fire. However, it was doubtful the enemy would waste ammunition on a single aircraft. Altitude would be no deterrent for the enemy fighters.

I turned to the course Columbus had given me, lowered the nose of the airplane slightly and pushed the remaining three engine throttles to climb power. Losing about 100 feet per minute we literally streaked for home at more than 200 mph.

Information on Tom was not good. He had lost a lot of blood and was unconscious. McCue was inert. The rest of the crew was busy keeping an eye out for enemy fighters. Fortunately, none were seen nor did any of them see us.

The combination of our "straight for home" course and higher speed allowed us to beat the Group home. As we turned on final, we fired a red-red flare. We touched down and rolled to the end of the runway and pulled off onto the taxi way where the Medics were waiting. They quickly climbed into the nose to check Tom. Among the Medical personnel meeting us was Dr. Jack.

In a short time, Dr. Jack came to me and said Tom did not make it. The shrapnel had severed his carotid artery. Jack said that even if he had been on board, Tom probably could not have been saved.

After Tom had been taken off the airplane, we started the engines and taxied back to the hard stand, shut the engines down and climbed out of the airplane. Still not believing what had happened, we spent time just walking around the airplane. Then, we saw how close we had all come. What must have been an 88 millimeter anti aircraft shell had gone through the left wing and left in its wake a hole about eight inches in diameter. It went through behind number 2 engine fuel tank and just ahead of the front edge of the left landing flap. Had the shell exploded either by its own fuse or by contact, the airplane would have been blown out of the sky in one fiery ball. Chance of survivors would have been nil.

When the shell passed through the wing, it cut away about half of the left flap torque tube. This is a cylindrical structural member about which the whole wing flap is constructed. This tube also carries the aerodynamic force when the flap is lowered. Given the severe damage inflicted upon the torque tube, it was amazing that it did not twist in two when we came in for our landing. Had that occurred, most of the left flap would have retracted and the aircraft most certainly would have slow rolled and gone in upside down on the final approach. Chance of survival? None.

We had been both very unlucky and very lucky that day, September 28, 1944. Thereafter, Thursdays would always be remembered by us as "Crash and Burn Day." We didn't; but we came mighty close.

Debriefing was a detached experience. Once debriefing was finished, it was time to return to the hut. However, to put the return off as long as possible, John, Columbus and I stopped in at the Officers' Club. Finally, all the reasons not to go back to our quarters were gone.

We walked in the front door of the hut fully expecting to see Tom sitting on his bed. Of course, he was not there. Also not there were his belongings. In the time it took us to get back to our quarters, the Squadron orderlies had come in and collected and taken away all of his belongings. It was as if he had never existed. It was just like the World War I aviation movies. Only this was not a movie it was for real.

That night, after a few more hours at the Officers' Club, fitful sleep was possible.

The next morning I went down to the Squadron C.O.'s office to see what happened next.

He said we had been removed from combat flight status for an indefinite time. This was no surprise. Tom would be buried at Cambridge American Military Cemetery within the next few days.

We could attend if we wished. That was easy to answer. We would go even though it involved a long, bumpy and cold journey in the back of a 6 X 6.

To let us unwind, we were given a 3 day pass with the suggestion that after the funeral we all go to London and see the "sights" and try to forget.

I told Major Pomeroy about McCue's behavior during the mission. Because of McCue's lack of response and action, which could have endangered the whole aircraft, I asked the Major to remove him immediately from the crew. To emphasize my feelings I told him I would not fly with McCue on the crew. Further, I recommended McCue be removed from flight status and grounded, permanently. The Major agreed immediately.

My concern now was that the crew might be broken up. After all, we didn't have a Copilot, an Engineer or a Radio Operator. The Major said Purdy would be put back on the crew to replace McCue. A fill-in Radio Operator would continue to cover until Hasselback was back on flight status. A Copilot would be assigned soon. Until a permanent one could be found, we would fly using an available copilot.

We attended Tom's funeral. It was a dark and windy day with a fine mist falling. The size of the cemetery was hard to believe. It seemed to extend for acres and acres. And there were rows upon rows of white crosses. Sure a somber and sobering sight.

The London trip was a real experience. The extent of the damage was unbelievable. It was far more extensive than what had been conveyed in the newsreels. However, what the newsreels hadn't gotten across was the way the people continued to carry on with little notice of the devastation around them. The British "stiff upper lip" was very apparent and obviously working well.

Aircraft bombing of London had practically stopped. It had been replaced by the V-1 Buzz Bomb and the V-2. The Buzz Bomb was similar to aircraft bombing in that its approach could be seen and/or heard. This allowed time for a warning to be sounded and time to take to cover. The V-2 was a different proposition. It struck without warning. Suddenly, there would be a terrific bang. One had hit. Although you might have not been very close to it, for the next several hours you would carry this thought, "What if I'm standing where the next one is aimed?". About the time this thought had faded from memory another V-2 would come in. And the "worry" cycle would restart. It was very damned unnerving.

In the evening, the subway platforms were used as bomb shelters. People were lying all about wrapped in blankets and quilts, most of them sleeping soundly. People and subway trains were moving by only a few feet away. This picture conveyed but one message: "Hitler, you're gonna lose this one! V-1's and V-2's will not do the job!. These people will never break!"

While in London I tried to find Tom's brother. He was a Second Lieutenant in the Field Artillery and had been wounded in the June 6th D-Day Invasion. Tom had planned to look him up at the first opportunity. As it turned out, because I had an insufficient address, I had no success in finding him.

When we got back from London, I became acquainted with a Pilot who lived in the hut across the "street". His name was Herbert D. Olson. He had been off on a "shuttle mission" when we arrived and had just returned. These missions involved flying from the U.K. to Russia to Italy and back to the U.K., bombing being done on each leg of the triangular route. He had engine engine trouble in Russia and had to drop out of the two return bombing missions. He made his way back to the 95th by flying through Teheran, Cairo and Rome.

We hit it off immediately. H.B. and his crew had also come to the 95th; however, they were placed in another Squadron which was

**THE AUTHOR AND HERB OLSON
A.K.A. "HIRED GUNS?"**

some distance from us. We saw each other occasionally. Usually at the Officers' Club.

Olson had gotten to the 95th only a short time before we did. For a 4 engine pilot he was on the small side. However, as the saying goes, "It's not the size of the dog in the fight. It's the size of the fight in the dog." This applied to Herb without modification. He was in Pearl Harbor when the Japs attacked. At the time, he was an enlisted Flight Engineer on a 17. As such, he flew his quota of missions out of Hawaii including the pivotal Battle of Midway. After that he returned to the States and completed Pilot Training.

Soon after we met, he suggested we go flying. Sounded like a good idea. He made a few phone calls and "Presto" —- there was an L-4B available to us. The L-4 was the military version of the very popular Piper Cub. Its cruise speed was less than the take off and landing speeds of the B-17. We spent an hour touring the area low and slow.

One day, Tom's brother came into the hut. He had heard about Tom's death and came up to get further information. We talked for a while and told him what had happened. He left us with the feeling he felt we had not done all that could/should have been done for Tom. We could not see what we could have done differently. Dr. Jack's words to us had confirmed that.

CHAPTER 14
BACK ON COMBAT STATUS

It was now almost two weeks since the first mission. On October 11, 1944 we were sent up for 2 1/2 hours on a practice mission and placed back on combat flight status. That accomplished, Operations lost no time. That night we were placed on alert for the October 12 mission. Our second mission was Bremen which was usually referred to as "Little B". Berlin, obviously, was "Big B". Our target was the railroad yards in the center of the city. Bremen was one of the more heavily defended targets; however, this time we were lucky and escaped with only minor flak damage to the airplane.

We flew two more missions in October. They were Cologne (target: railroad yards) and Munster (target: airfield). Both missions were easy ones. We now had four missions under our belt.

Robert "Mac" S. McCoy had joined the crew as Copilot. He, like Tom, had hoped to be a fighter Pilot, but Uncle Sam had different ideas and plans. Except for the desire to be a fighter Pilot, Mac and Tom were totally different. Tom was quiet. Mac was anything but. Mac wore his cap on the back of his head like "Hot Shot Charlie" and seemed to know no fear. He also had little tolerance or respect for rank.

Again, unlike Tom, he did like to drink, a thing he did with considerable gusto. One night at the Officers' Club he put on a pretty good load. When he returned from the Club to the hut, he thought there were rats running around in between the hut walls. (Probably correct. It had happened before.) What better to do than to eradicate same rats by use of his 45 pistol? It took only one shot to empty the hut of people. And, they left in a big hurry. The rats were untouched. Fortunately, the holes in the roof were over his bed.

| **ROBERT MCCOY,** | **JOHN INGLEMAN,** |
| **COPILOT** | **BOMBARDIER** |

George Hail climbed my frame for not having my crew under better control. I told George I was not about to throw rank on a drunk with a loaded 45 in his hand. Particularly, one who didn't have much, if any respect for rank. End of discussion.

After Mac sobered up, I did "take a strip" off his hide. Fortunately, there were no repeat "performances."

Then came November 2, 1944. We were alerted.

The briefing was an unexpected and unwelcome shock. Number 5 was going to be MERSEBURG!!

This was unbelievable. ONE OF THE MOST HEAVILY DEFENDED TARGETS IN GERMANY TWICE IN OUR FIRST FIVE MISSIONS!!

When we ran up the engines prior to take off, two of them had slightly greater than the normally allowable rpm drop when switched to one magneto. A tailor made and an acceptable reason to abort.

Mac, Jim and I had a brief discussion and came to the conclusion the problem was not serious enough to keep us on the ground. We'd keep an eye on them, and if more serious trouble appeared, we'd take action then. Mac, Jim and I held this discussion on the intercom; therefore, the rest of the crew had taken it all in not missing a single detail. Several times, as we flew on to the target, someone would come on the intercom and ask, "How are the mags doing? Shouldn't we go back?" The reply: "Everything's fine. We're going on."

I was tempted to abort but could not bring myself to do it. If I bought off on this legitimate, although flimsy, excuse, would I then begin to see boogie men behind every tree? And, certainly it would set a bad example for those who had trusted and stuck with me in the past. Once this doubt was put behind, it was business as "usual".

We bored on towards Merseburg. Needless to say, everyone on board was as tight as a fiddle string. As we left the I.P. and headed towards the target, flak was as heavy and menacing as it had been the first time. In fact, it even seemed to be heavier.

Although we lost an engine to flak damage over the target, the rest of the airplane suffered little damage and no one was hit. This time we lost number 2 engine. A piece of shrapnel went through the oil cooler and created a major leak. As before, the engine was shut down and the prop feathered before all the oil was lost.

This incident brought home how really cold it was at these altitudes. After the oil cooler was hit, the hot oil started to leak out the hole the piece of flak had made when it exited through the top of the leading edge of the wing. As the oil came out of the hole, instead of being blown back over the top of the wing and lost in the sky behind us, it began to pile up like an ant hill of black tar. Even the 200 mile per hour plus wind passing over the wing couldn't blow it

"COME ON, GUYS, LET'S GET THIS FORMATION TIGHTENED UP!"

away. The "black ant hill" stayed there until we neared the base and descended to lower altitude and warmer temperatures. Then, it did the expected; turned liquid and was blown back over the top of the wing and disappeared.

Unlike the first trip to Merseburg, we did not lose the formation this day. We came back with the rest of the Group.

159

The next three missions, in order, were: Nuenkirchen (coke plant); Neumunster (railroad yards) and Saarbrucken (railroad yards). On these three raids there was little flak and, in general, they were considered "milk runs" —- that is, just as uneventful as going to the store for a bottle of milk. On the first one of these missions, the lead bombardier couldn't find the target so we brought the bombs back with us. A rather dumb bit of action, we all thought and said. On the Saarbrucken raid we carried our biggest bomb load to date. Six 1,000 pound general purpose or demolition bombs. Previously, our loads had been in the 5,000 pound range.

We were now veterans of eight missions and holder of the Air Medal which had been awarded upon the completion of six missions. Only 27 more to go. That is, unless 8th Air Force Command raised the number from 35 to something more. Like, 50, the number required by the 15th Air Force in Italy.

CHAPTER 15
THINGS OTHER THAN COMBAT

It was mid November. Olson and I had by now become close friends and spent most of our free time together.

In order to occupy our spare time, Olson and I violated one of the cardinal rules of the Army. We volunteered!! We informed the Squadron Engineering Officer that we would be willing to "slow time" combat aircraft for him. This entailed flying, at low power settings and speed, aircraft which had just had one or more engines changed. With a crew of three (Pilot, Copilot and Engineer) the lightly loaded plane was flown at reduced speed for a couple of hours, usually in the vicinity of the base. This allowed the new parts in the recently overhauled engines to "wear in" before being subjected to the stresses of combat flying. We took turns as Pilot and Copilot on these flights.

At times we had difficulty in finding a volunteer Engineer, so more than once we used our room orderly, "Alabama", as Flight Engineer. He didn't know anything about the airplane but he liked to fly.

On one of our slow time flights we were asked to fly a crew to the west coast of England so they could catch a flight back to the States. On this flight, Olson was the Pilot. He got the plane off the ground and to our cruising altitude of about 1,500 feet. He eased the power back to cruise and trimmed the flight controls to the "hands off" condition. Shortly, the airplane started to climb. He retrimmed it to level flight. But, then it started to dive. Again he retrimmed. Still the "nose up" and the "nose down" cycle continued. We wondered if, when changing the engines, they also in some way had messed up the aircraft controls.

Given Alabama's lack of B-17 knowledge, I said I'd go back through the fuselage and check the elevator control cables to see if there was something interfering with them and causing our problem.

When I looked out the back door of the radio room toward the tail end of the aircraft, I saw the problem. Our "passengers" had a crap game in progress. They would throw the dice on the catwalk to the rear of the airplane. Then they would move to the back to read the dice. The next throw of the dice would be forward along the catwalk, and they then walked forward to check the dice. I went back to the cockpit and told Olson he was going to have to hand fly the thing until we got rid of our passengers. The importance of the crap game outweighed his inconvenience.

As we approached our destination, I called the tower for landing instructions. The tower came back with the requested info and a question: "Do you have any VIP on board?" This was the first time I'd heard that acronym. Thinking it referred to some secret radio or radar equipment, I told the tower I'd check and see. I asked Olson what VIP was. He didn't know either. I called the tower back and said we didn't have any.

We landed and taxied up to the tower to unload our passengers. As soon as the props stopped, we were descended upon by three staff cars and hordes of people all of whom were in Class A uniforms and shiny shoes.

We found out they were expecting a visit from some very high level brass and thought we were them. They had interpreted my delay in replying to their question as an attempt to make them think that the brass wasn't aboard. That's how we learned VIP meant Very Important Person and that it did not refer to some deep, dark war secret.

Due to our dress (class "scroungy"), Olson, Alabama and I were loaded onto a 6 X 6 truck and taken to a remote part of the base for lunch. The base commanders certainly didn't want the visiting brass to see us and come to the conclusion we were part of their operation. We did, however, have a good lunch —- steak, in fact. While we were having lunch the General did show up, so the Base personnel got to strut their stuff. After the General's visit was over and he had left, they let us return to the airplane and fly back to Horham.

Olson and I had been in London a number of times; so, this is a good a point as any to relate the "Tales of London".

About every three weeks we were given a two day pass. If the finances could stand it, this usually meant a trip to London.

The nearby towns were all rather drab and uninteresting, while, on the other hand, London had lots of things going on.

The trip to London was fairly quick and easy. The Group ran a shuttle service with a 2 1/2 Ton truck between the base and the railroad station at Eye. The trains were almost always full so we oft times spent the whole trip standing up. We didn't carry baggage, as such. We did take a musette bag with a change of underwear and socks, a clean shirt and toilet articles. We were also required to carry our gas mask.

Ingenuity soon asserted itself. The bag for the gas mask was quite a bit smaller than the musette bag. Since our limited traveling equipment would fit in the gas mask bag (without the mask in it), we removed the gas mask from its bag and substituted the contents of the musette bag. The musette bag was left at the base. This stroke of genius reduced the size and weight of the load we had to drag along.

However, there was a downside. For instance, when M.P.'s stopped us in the train station in London and asked to inspect gas masks. We were soon to find out that this little run-in resulted in a report to the base commander with the implication that proper disciplinary action be taken. The Squadron C.O. called us in and said something like, "You really ought to carry the gas mask when you are going to run into M.P.'s." End of incident. Thereafter, we were on the lookout for M.P.'s when going to London. We always had our "gas mask" with us.

Piccadilly Circus was the major center of activity in London. At night, the sidewalks around the cement barricaded statue of Eros were heavily populated by girls. The word "girls" could be changed to "whores" without erroneously describing the scene and only slandering a very few.

Due to the total blackout, the streets were pitch black at night. This prompted the girls to adopt the technique of carrying pen flashlights. As a Serviceman walked by, the "girls" would shine the light in his face. If they liked what they saw, an offer would be forthcoming. The "offer" might be a "quickie" in a near by close (alley) to an "all nighter" in her apartment. Just as the offers varied so did the prices. From about 2 Pounds ($8.70) for a "quickie" to 10 Pounds ($43.50) for all night.

Neither Olson nor I ever succumbed to these enticements, although there was one night when we came awfully close. We were accosted by twins. In fact, very good looking blondes. We started serious negotiations, and it looked like we had a real good deal at five Pounds, each. Before the deal was clinched (pun intended) we were informed that the just negotiated price was for a "quickie" in a nearby close. At that, the deal went soft, literally, and was terminated right then and there.

My Aunt Miriam had visited England before the War and in the course of her visit made friends with a Mrs. Monk. Mrs. Monk may have been a school teacher as was Aunt Miriam. Aunt Miriam had written Mrs. Monk and told her I was stationed in England and, in turn, Aunt Miriam had written me, if an opportunity presented itself, to visit Mrs. Monk. So, on one of our trips to London, Olson and I searched for and found her. I called her to ask if it was O.K. for us to come out. It was.

We, by now, had been to London often enough to figure out how to use the subway (in English, the Tube or the Underground) and the buses. Her home was quite a way outside of London, however, we found it with no difficulty. She welcomed us with open arms and we spent a couple of hours in conversation over tea and some freshly baked cup cakes. The plate piled high with cup cakes was a temptation for Olson and me. They were very good. However, we realized these cup cakes probably represented at least a month's or more sugar ration. We used restraint and stopped at two each. It was an enjoyable visit. I only hope that we didn't eat too much.

Our trips to London did not consist solely of walking around Piccadilly Circus, frequently referred to as the "meat market" for obvious reasons. The movie houses and the theatres, although their marquees were dark, were very much in operation. Among the shows we saw were "Arsenic and Old Lace" (new at the time), "Strike it Again" with Sid Field, "Is Your Honeymoon Really Necessary?" and Sir Lawrence Olivier's "Henry the Fifth". This latter film was most spectacular for two reasons. First, it was in Technicolor (still somewhat novel in 1944) and second, because it had been made in wartime England.

Our usual base in London was the Red Cross Club in Kensington. The beds were good, the place was clean and food was available. However, one of the meals we had there was a disaster, for us. It was fish. It looked delicious and the serving was more than ample. What was wrong? It was <u>COD</u>!!! It tasted like it had been drenched in cod liver oil. Struggle as we could, the stuff just wouldn't go down with any assurance it would stay there. It pained us quite a lot to leave it essentially untouched since we knew how short food was. From then on, we always made sure and asked what the entre was before we ordered.

Speaking of food, the U.S. Army had taken over Grosvenor House, one of London's premier hotels on Park Lane overlooking Hyde Park. The ball rooms had been converted into Officers' Messes. In making the conversion, the masses were divided by rank. The largest, of course, was for Company Grade (Warrant Officer through Captain). Next, was for Field Grade (Major through Colonel) and last, but by no means the least, was a mess hall for Generals only. We never saw so many Officers in our life. The place was nicknamed "Willow Run" after the huge Ford Motor Company B-24 assembly plant outside Detroit.

There were a number of private clubs in London. Private meant that you had to be a member to get in. Of course, memberships were available and readily obtained for a few pounds. The clubs had booze, a little food, sometimes a floor show, music and occasionally, girls (available, for a price). One of the many things to watch out for was bogus booze. One time, after being approached on the street, Mac bought a bottle of Scotch for 3 Pounds (about $12.00) which turned out to be weak tea. It was reported, on some occasions of on-the-street purchases, the bottle's contents turned out to be "used tea". The color was close.

The V-2's continued to rain down on London. In spite of our combat experience, our fear and apprehension were the same as our first encounter with these things a couple of months previously. That is, we wondered, "Where is the next one going to hit?" for the several hours following the last explosion. About the time that thought faded into history, here comes another one of the damn things. The damage to buildings, streets and other things, from what we saw, was not all that great; however, these things had a great psychological effect.

LONDON THEATRE PROGRAMS

and

LONDON CLUB MEMBERSHIP CARDS

After an evening at the show or club (not, pub) crawling, we would usually stop by Lyon's Corner House for a late evening snack. On one such evening Olson and I went there. We sat on one side of a table for four. We had been there but a few minutes when a girl came up to the table and sat down across from Olson. She immediately began to work on him to provide her with some refreshments. Implied, was that she would reciprocate with refreshments or entertainments of her own. Olson was uninterested in both aspects of the deal and he told her so. She persisted. Finally, Olson, in his characteristically direct manner said, "Get lost, you two-bit whore." She did not take kindly to this suggestion and expressed her displeasure by picking up the place setting of silverware and throwing it with considerable force towards Olson's head. He ducked most of it, but one or more pieces hit him in the forehead and inflicted a small cut. As cuts to the head usually do, this one bled considerably. The sight of so much blood panicked the girl, and she took off running and went out the door.

Blood had been spilled; therefore, needless to say, Olson and I were in hot pursuit. As we exited the restaurant, we were joined by a couple of the Enlisted Men from Olson's crew who just happened to be passing by.

The four of us caught up with the girl by a bombed out building which had been secured by a board fence. We surrounded her and started to lecture about how impolite it was to attack Officers of the U.S. Army Air Force who were in England trying to protect the British from the Nazis. The lecture was proceeding in a polite, but firm, matter-of-fact fashion, when one of Olson's crew members, with considerable conviction, said, "No slut's gonna hit MY Pilot". He followed this up with a strong right jab direct to the girl's chin. The crack of the punch to the chin was followed by a pronounced "thump" as the back of her head rebounded off the board fence.

Her immediate response was to yell "Bobby!! Bobby!!". This brought the lecture series to a quick halt. We told the E.M. to get lost because if there was trouble about the incident, they could lose their stripes. More than likely, if it was reported, all Olson and I would get out of it would be a reprimand and possibly a fine.

As we started to depart the scene, it dawned upon Olson and me that, in our haste to pursue, we had left our service caps and trench coats on the coat rack in Lyon's Corner House. We decided to take a circuitous route back to the place and retrieve them. When we arrived at the entrance, a fairly large crowd had gathered. In the center of the crowd was the girl excitedly talking with a couple of Bobbies. Olson and I, inconspicuously as possible, worked our way around the edge of the crowd and reclaimed our belongings. Continuing to try to keep a low profile, we eased our way out the door and started toward the safety of the blackout. Then, just as we thought we had it made, the girl saw us and yelled, "There they are!!!". Suddenly, we went from being on the fringes of the crowd to being in the center of it. And things really were not going well for us.

As if on cue, a station wagon with two burly U.S. Navy Shore Patrol Petty Officers pulled up to the curb.

Olson and I now knew how the settlers felt, when, just as the Indians had circled the wagons, the Cavalry came over the hill.

One of the S.P.'s boomed out, "What's going on here?". A Bobby explained the situation, as he knew it, to the S.P. The S.P. said, "Just leave it to us. We'll take care of these two." He then turned to us and said, "Sirs, will you please get in the back of the wagon." We almost ran and jumped in.

As the station wagon pulled away from the curb, the S.P. turned around and asked, "Was that whore giving you a bad time, Sirs?" Then, "Where are you staying, sirs, we'll drop you off there."

End of another incident. Whew!!

General officers in the Army had considerable leeway when it came to the styling of their uniforms. General George S. Patton was one who exercised this prerogative in a rather flamboyant manner.

His dress (Class A) uniform included a chrome plated helmet, two pearl handled six-shooters and riding breeches and boots. General Eisenhower, shortly after arriving in the ETO, expressed his individualism by adopting a version of the British battle jacket for his dress uniform —- which came to be called the Eisenhower Battle Jacket.

A number of U.S. Army types viewed this waist length jacket as a much more sensible garment than the regulation finger tip length blouse. The blouse with its liberal dose of brass buttons and large patch pockets, which you couldn't use, was viewed as being somewhat of a waste of both brass and very good cloth.

Seeing Ike's jacket, someone must have rationalized, "If Ike can do it, so can I. After all, the U.S. is supposed to be a democracy." Soon, scores of both Officers and Enlisted Men (mostly Air Force types) had "Eisenhower Battle Jackets" made and were wearing them. No one said you couldn't do it; so, soon battle jacketed personnel out numbered those wearing blouses.

Naturally, I had to have one, too. Consequently, on a trip to London I went to Bond Street to find a tailor who would make me a battle jacket. With no difficulty, I found Raman's at 10 New Bond Street who was very willing to satisfy my clothing desire.

He took my measurements, a 50% deposit and said I could pick it up in a couple of fortnights. On my next leave, I returned to London, picked up my battle jacket and joined the rest of the elite. I've forgotten how much I paid for it; however, the sum of 20 pounds ($85.00) comes to mind. When I ordered the jacket, there was no question but what I would be able to come back and pick it up. Oh! The self assurance and invincibility of youth! Obviously, the tailor also thought I would be back to pick it up. On the other hand, maybe, the 50% deposit covered his costs, plus.

Back at the base. It would be less than truthful to say that the partaking of alcoholic beverages occurred mostly off of the base. There was more than a fair amount of drinking on the base. The two main locations were the Officers' and Enlisted Men's Clubs and in the huts. However, in our particular hut, while there was usually a bottle or two available, I never saw any serious drinking taking place there. One additional on-base rendezvous a chosen few of us discovered was a most unlikely one, the base hospital. The 412th Flight Surgeon, one Captain Sanford, made this possible. The good Captain not only had a thirst for the stuff but also had access to the store of G.I. "medicinal" spirits. This led to several parties in the hospital. On one occasion the party did get a bit raucous resulting in complaints being registered by the patients. So that no one thinks we were insensitive to the needs of the patients, most of the patients were there because of such ailments as colds, minor injuries or less serious wounds. The serious cases were sent to nearby General Hospitals. However, these complaints ended these parties.

The Officers' Club had the very necessary bar plus a number of four person booths along one of the walls. A few tables scattered about the rest of the room completed the furnishings. Adjoining the bar was a lounge with an assortment of tables, some sofas and overstuffed chairs and lamp tables. Drinks were not served in the lounge; however, they could be brought in to the lounge from the bar.

For the Saturday night dance, the Lounge furniture was cleared out, and it became the "ballroom". There were also several card rooms which were usually in use every night for no limit poker games. I never sat in on these card games at the Club. They were just too rich for my blood. The games were "no limit"; thus, the Majors and Lt. Colonels, with their superior resources, could and often did, "buy" the pot by a series of big raises which the lower ranks couldn't equal.

171

Columbus was more or less a frequent participant in these games. He usually won. Not big, but enough so he was able to come back to the hut and let us take it away from him in penny ante games.

At the Club, Olson and I preferred the beer to the hard stuff. In a relatively short time, we laid claim to a regular booth. This led to the creation of a "game", that came to be known as the "Double Pyramid". Of course, Olson and I weren't the only "players" —- others would join us to help reach the game's goal. This help was much appreciated; particularly, if the game "assistants" would buy us one, too.

The objective of the game was to assemble a double pyramid of beer bottles on the table in the booth —- an arrangement which would extend from the wall toward the aisle. As each bottle was emptied, it was not returned to the bar to be replaced by a full one. Instead, it was "stockpiled" on the table. When the "game" ended, from above, the "playing board" with the "Double Pyramid" appeared thus:

```
                              O                    O
                                O                O
       A                     O    O           O    O
       S                       O    O    O    O              W
       I                     O    O    O    O    O            A
       L                       O    O    O    O              L
       E                     O    O           O    O          L
                                O                O
                              O                    O
```

When this configuration was achieved, the "game" was over and it was time to head for the hut. Often, the objective was reached before the next day's mission alert was posted or the bar closed.

When the Group was placed on alert for a mission, the first step was to hoist a red flag ("Maggie's Drawers") on the flag pole outside of Headquarters. Shortly after, the word would be passed to the Officers' and the Enlisted Men's Club bars, and they were immediately closed down.

There were times when the alert came down rather late, causing the bar closing to be pretty close to the time for the departure of the mission. For some, this could result in a not too sober take off.

After some serious thought on this state of affairs, Olson and I came up with a suitable antidote. Hot Chocolate. It soon became a ritual for us to stop off in the Squadron Headquarters Hut on the way back to our huts and make two canteen cups of hot chocolate. One for each of us. I had written Mother and asked her if it was possible to send me some cocoa —- which she did. Once the cocoa arrived, from there on it was simple. "Appropriate" the necessary "iron cow" (condensed milk) and sugar from the Officers' Mess to fill out the required list of ingredients. The Squadron Headquarters hut was chosen as the preparation site since they could always be counted on to have a fire in the stove. This potion really did clear our heads for the next day's "work".

I still remember the recipe for the hot chocolate. Place four heaping tablespoons each of cocoa and sugar into the canteen cup and fill it one half full of water. Put the cup on the stove and bring the contents to a boil; stir until the contents are reduced to about one third a cup. Add one can of condensed milk and stir it in. Allow the cup to heat, stirring occasionally until small bubbles begin to appear on the top surface around the edge. Remove from the stove, sip carefully and enjoy it. It is more than likely this concoction will not taste as good if it is not made in a canteen cup and on a coke fired pot bellied stove. More than likely, the Nissen hut is not required.

On one particular night, November 15, the alert was not posted until very late in the evening. Unfortunately, at the time we received the information, Olson and I, and others had reached the "game's" objective. In spite of the hot chocolate, the late alert and the "game" combined to set the stage for a difficult day.

More about that, next.

CHAPTER 16
MORE COMBAT

It seemed like I had no more than hit the sack than the Orderly was rousting us out. Today's target was a gun emplacement just across the lines. Mission number 9 was going to be a real milk run, if there ever was one. About all we had to do was to get close to the lines, "pitch" the bombs across the lines and head for home. More than likely, we wouldn't see a single burst of flak. That is, of course, unless our own people shot at us. This was always a threat when we operated near the front line. Certainly, there would be no enemy fighters to worry about today.

After take off and a short climb, we slipped into our place in the formation. By then, the effects of the long evening and short sleep were beginning to tell on me; I told Mac to take over while I had a brief nap. I asked him to wake me up when we got near the Initial Point (I.P.) for the beginning of our bombing run for the target.

All too soon, he woke me and said we were not too far from the I.P. The little nap had been most refreshing; however, as frequently happens after a nap, a certain internal pressure had built up — undoubtedly some residual fluid from the previous night's "double pyramid game" at the Officers' Club. I asked Columbus to pass up the hydraulic can. John came back with: "Can you hold it for a little bit; we're practically on the I.P. now."

I told him I thought so, but to pass the can up anyway so it would close at hand.

As expected, the antiaircraft fire was practically non-existent. There were a few bursts "here" and "there". However, just after the bombs were dropped and we went into a steep diving right hand turn toward the Rally Point, one of the "here's" was real close underneath our airplane.

A couple of pieces of shrapnel "thumped" through the bottom of the airplane just ahead of my feet and behind Columbus' position. One of these pieces clipped the hydraulic brake line just in front of my right foot. Immediately, I was hit full in the face with a stream of hydraulic fluid.

I had the controls as we made the evasive steep diving turn to the right. With the hydraulic fluid squirting on my sun glasses I couldn't see a thing. I waved to Mac to take over. For some reason or other, my predicament struck him as the greatest joke in the world and he doubled up laughing.

Finally, his humor controlled, he took over. By now the hydraulic lines were empty and the squirting stopped. If pure oxygen comes into contact with oil under the right conditions, the oil may burst into flames. My big concern now was that hydraulic fluid would come into contact with the oxygen in my mask and result in an even bigger problem. I quickly got the fluid wiped off my glasses and oxygen mask and eliminated that concern. However, the area of confusion now moved into the nose compartment. From his location, John could not see the color of the hydraulic fluid. So, he came over the intercom with: "John, you didn't piss in the airplane, did you?"

Before I could reply, Columbus, confusing red hydraulic with another body fluid, came on with "That's BLOOD! THEY'VE HIT

PIECES OF FLAK
ONE OF THESE CUT THE BRAKE LINE
MISSION NUMBER NINE

JOHN!" In retrospect, I've wondered if Columbus thought my blood was really that thin and pale colored. On the other hand, he may have been making allowances for my previous night's activities.

Soon calm was restored. And, none too soon, the hydraulic can was put to use.

I asked Purdy to check and see if there was some way to plug the hole in the brake line. After a while he came back and said there was nothing on board which would serve as a patch to hold the 2000 psi hydraulic pressure. This meant we had no brakes and couldn't operate the cowl flaps. The latter was no big deal; however, the other was. It was a BIG problem. Landing with no brakes could be more than a little interesting.

This point may be raised: If you had been able to patch the hydraulic line did you carry spare hydraulic fluid in the airplane? No, we didn't carry spare hydraulic fluid. But, we did have one or more hydraulic fluid cans which had fluid in them. In a pinch, this fluid would work. However, only if the altitude was low enough and the temperature warm enough so the fluid was fluid and not ice. This remedy had been used before.

The Group headed for home. We were about half way across the Channel when the Lead came on the horn with the news that our base was socked in solid and we were being diverted to an alternate field. This was more unwelcome news. We would have to land with no brakes on a strange field.

It developed that our alternate was a Troop Carrier field in southern England.

When we came into sight of the field, the news got even worse. Along the right side of the main runway, about 100 feet from the edge, were C-47's lined up wing tip to wing tip. Lined up on the left side, in the same manner, were CG-4 Gliders. If we ran off the runway, no matter which side, we stood a damn good chance to wipe out either a bunch of C-47's or CG-4's. Plowing in to either of them would make our stopping even more spectacular and memorable than would either a simple ground loop or with the airplane's tail in the air and the nose in the ground.

I called our Lead and the Tower and told them of our predicament and that we would wait until everybody else was down before we tried to land. Thus, if we made a mess of things and closed the airfield, at least the rest of the Group's airplanes would be on the ground. This would also give us time to burn off some more of our fuel load. The smaller the amount of fuel we had on board, the smaller would be the size of the fire should something untoward happen.

We circled the field as the rest of the Group landed. While we circled, I asked George and Larry to see if they could rig a parachute so it could be deployed out of the radio room hatch after we landed. This would help to slow us down. After a little time, they said that by using the safety ropes along the bomb bay catwalk, this could be done. I told them to proceed.

All too soon, our turn to land came. Emergency equipment was lined up just off of the approach end of the runway and a number of spectators could be seen lining the ramp. Obviously someone had passed the word, and they were waiting for the "show" to begin. Now it was time. We lined up on the runway, dropped full flaps and pulled the power back to the point where we were just hanging in the air. The airspeed was only one or two miles an hour above stalling. We crossed the end of the runway with no more than 20 feet of air underneath us. Pulled the power off. Then began what seemed to be an interminable time for the bird to quit flying and touch down. Soon the mains kissed the runway.

Now, it was decision time. Would another approach leave us with more runway? Were we lined up well enough with the center of the runway? Had we made the right allowance for any cross wind? After a quick assessment of these issues, it seemed doubtful that we could do better with another approach. Thus, I told Mac to kill all four engines. He did. However, out of habit, after he placed the fuel mixture controls in "cut-off", he pushed all four throttles forward. The small amount of fuel remaining in the carburetors gave a little boost to our speed, which was the very last thing we needed. But it was too late to do anything about it now. No way could we get all four fans started and get enough speed to fly before the end of the runway was reached. NO DOUBT!! We HAD landed!!

God, it was quiet as we rolled down the runway with the engines shut off. Told the fellows in the radio room to pop the chute. Felt a little backward tug as they did.

As we continued to roll along the runway, the only sounds were the thumping as the main landing gear struts occasionally bottomed and the drum-like sounds as the fuselage panels flexed like the bottoms of so many oil cans.

I held the tail up as long as possible to milk the last bit of directional control out of that barn door of a rudder. Now we had slowed to the point where the rudder had absolutely no effect. It was time to pull back on the control column to set the tail on the runway and get as much drag out of the elevators as possible.

Without any way to steer, we began to drift to the left side of the runway towards the CG-4's. Out of the two choices the CG-4's were the best. They weren't as solidly built as the C-47's PLUS they didn't have gasoline tanks!! Nothing could be done about changing our direction now. Too little time remained to start #1 or #2 to return us to the runway center line. Even if we did, the resulting increase in speed would probably send us off the end of the runway.

Finally, we stopped. The left main was just about 2 feet from the left edge of the runway. About 300 feet of runway remained ahead of us. It had been close.

Several years later there would be a sequel to this story. While attending the University of Southern California, a group of us "War Heroes" were telling war stories over lunch. Came my turn and I told the story of this incident. One of the fellows in the group, John Regus, said, "Hey!! I remember that! I was stationed at that field as a C-47 pilot." Small World.

It turned out the parachute was not as effective as it could have been. This, for the simple reason that I had George and Larry pop it too soon. Our speed was too great so it tore away rather quickly. However, it was not a total loss. It was no longer suitable for its originally intended use. The remains were divided up among the crew for souvenirs. But, it did make really nice scarves.

MAJOR JIM FRANKOWSKY
C.O. 412TH BOMB SQUADRON

We spent the night there. IN A TENT!!! During the night, the airplane was fixed and we flew back to our base the next morning with the rest of the Group.

When we got back good news was waiting. I had been promoted to First Lieutenant. This would certainly help the cash situation.

It was also around this time that Charlie, the tail gunner, went AWOL. The Squadron C.O., now Major Frankowsky, one morning called me in and told me Charlie was missing. I said I thought he was probably somewhere nearby. The Major said, if that was the case, I better go find him. He said he would give me a jeep and a driver for the hunt. After traversing the nearby roads for some little time, we went by a farm house and there was Charlie's bicycle leaning up against it. I went to the door of the house and knocked. Sure enough, Charlie was there. I told him to get his bike and himself in the back seat of the jeep RIGHT NOW!!

Upon return to the base we went in to see the Major. The Major lectured Charlie on the error of his ways. He then turned to me and asked what punishment should be handed down. Reduced in rank? Taken off of flight status? Removed from the crew?

I told him Charlie was a fine tail gunner, and I did not want to give him up. However, he had broken regulations and for that some punishment was due. Charlie was broken from Staff Sergeant to Private. However, after a couple of missions, I began pushing to have him promoted. In a short time he was back up to Staff Sergeant.

The next mission was number 10. It was a milk run. This could have been because both the Lead Navigator and the Bombardier got lost.

So, on Sunday, November 26, 1944, as the good citizens of Gutersloh, Germany made their way to church, they probably noticed a formation of B-17's, with the sun glinting off the wings, high overhead. Their thoughts could have been: "Those poor souls in Hamm are in for another good pasting today. Gott in Himmel!"

They should have saved their pity. Because little old Gutersloh, not Hamm, was the unintended target of the 95th that day.

How this happened was a mystery. There was hardly a cloud in the sky and, while Gutersloh and the intended target were similar, there were enough readily identifiable differences to distinguish between them. I guess the citizens of Gutersloh, while not knowing of him, understood what General Sherman meant when he said, "War is Hell."

A few days later we were again placed on alert. The morning of November 30, 1944 came and, as the curtain covering the Briefing Room map was parted, we were faced again with that dreaded word, "Merseburg". To be sent to the same target for the third time in 11 missions seemed unreal. Also, more than grossly unfair.

All too soon, the briefing was finished. We climbed aboard the airplane. Engines were started. We took off. Climbed to assembly altitude. The Group formation pulled itself together and we were on our way to Germany.

When the crew was on oxygen, which was required above 10,000 feet, it was standard procedure for either the Copilot or the Pilot, which ever one was not flying the airplane, to call each crew member every 10 minutes to remind him to check his oxygen supply. This was necessary as an individual seldom recognizes that he is not receiving oxygen. Just before we turned towards the I.P., Mac made an oxygen check.

All reported O.K.

Although we were at 30,000 feet, the flak over Merseburg was as murderous as it had been the two previous times. However, this time we came through with all four engines still running and very little damage.

As we headed to the Rally Point, Mac made another oxygen check. Everyone reported in O.K. except Columbus. There was no response.

Mac asked John to check him out.

Shortly, John came back and said, "He seems to be passed out; however, I don't see any sign of a wound."

After a few moments, John said, "His oxygen hose isn't hooked up to the regulator!!"

John got a walk-around oxygen bottle, turned the regulator to pure oxygen and tried to get Nelson breathing again. In the meantime, having completed the bomb run, we and the Group headed toward home.

Mac joined John down in the nose compartment and both kept working on Nelson. But with no success. There was no question: he was dead.

As we neared the halfway point on the way back, it became apparent that in trying to revive Nelson, our oxygen supply had been greatly reduced and was nearing depletion. We were going to be forced to leave the formation and go to a lower altitude and head for home alone. Which is what we did.

This mission has always bothered me. Even more than the first one. For the simple reason that Nelson's death was totally unnecessary. It would have been avoided if the oxygen hose had been properly fastened to the regulator. It might have been avoided if oxygen checks had been either more often or more detailed. Perhaps Nelson was too preoccupied with outside goings on to check his oxygen regulator when called to make an oxygen check.

After return to base we examined Nelson's log. It was apparent that for some distance before the I.P., his handwriting had begun to deteriorate. It became more illegible from that time on until about halfway between the I.P. and the target. At that point it trailed off into just a wavy line and then stopped. This told us he had responded to at least two crew oxygen checks. Needless to say, I recalled very vividly the altitude chamber "ride" at Santa Ana during Preflight training.

The Navigator's regulator is mounted on the rear bulkhead of the nose compartment and to the left side of his desk. More than likely, Nelson had been looking out either the nose side windows or the front watching for enemy action and keeping track of our position. Thus, to check the regulator, he had to turn and look to the rear of the airplane.

He must have failed to do this. (The oxygen regulator has a flow indicator which looks like a pair of lips. When connected to the mask, the "lips" open and close with each breath the mask wearer takes.) With the hose disconnected from the regulator the "lips" would not have been moving with each breath. Also, more than likely, if he had checked the regulator flow indicator, the disconnected hose could be seen easily.

For the second time in little over two months, we made the very sad journey to the American Military Cemetery at Cambridge.

Ironically, Nelson had just been before the evaluation board for a promotion from Flight Officer to a Second Lieutenant. I felt he had a good chance of making it.

We were taken off combat status for a week. The Squadron C.O. told me there were no unassigned Navigators available. He suggested John take over the navigating duties. An enlisted "Togglier" would then be assigned to take over the Bombardier's duties. This proposal made sense for several reasons. A part of John's Bombardier training included navigation; thus, he was a very capable Navigator.

Further, only a few of the ships in the Group ever carried a bomb sight. Usually only the Squadron lead and his number 2 man (on the right wing) were equipped with the Norden bomb sight. Thus, in operation, the Lead aircraft would drop his bombs and the Bombardiers in the rest of the Squadron would release their bombs when they saw the lead aircraft bombs dropping. Thus the Bombardier's skills were not really needed except in the Squadron Lead and his right wing man aircraft.

Because of this, the position of Bombardier was often taken by "Toggliers", usually an unassigned gunner.

I made the proposal to John. His response was a quick and definite "NO". John didn't give a reason for his decision, and I didn't press for one. True, he, depending upon your viewpoint, did have the "best seat in the house". That is, if you like seeing the path ahead of you "decorated" with an over abundance of greasy black flak bursts.

I relayed John's response to the C.O. and told him I did not feel like forcing John to take the Navigator's position. The C.O. gave me no argument. So, for the 12th through the 35th we few with an assortment of enlisted Navigators. I must confess, I do not recall the name of a single one of them. Nor could any of the remaining crew members when I asked them a few years ago.

Regulations specified that Officers and Enlisted Men lead separate lives off duty. For this reason, neither John, Mac, Nelson nor I associated much with the Enlisted Men on our crew. Also, none of the "Navigators" wanted to move in with the rest of the crew members. So, the only time we were together was while flying and that did not lend itself to the establishment of friendships.

After a week off, we went back on combat status. Operations really worked us out this time. We flew three days in a row. This was the first time that had happened. The first two of the three were milk runs. The third one brought us our first abort. Number four prop kept running away, and we could not get it under control. This was a situation too fraught with the possibility of serious damage to the aircraft for us to attempt to go on. Fortunately, we were far enough into the mission for it to count as one of our required thirty five.

Later on in our tour we were "privileged" to see what happens when a prop comes off an engine. We were on our way home one day when we noticed a lone B-17 to the right and a bit above and ahead of us. Judging from the oil being lost he apparently had taken a hit in number four engine and could not get it feathered. As we watched, the prop and the engine nose section came off and flew out ahead of and slightly to the right of the airplane for a short distance. It then climbed a hundred feet or so and slowly rolled so the plane of the blades was parallel to the ground. Fortunately, it climbed high enough so it missed the wing. From there on it began to fall to the ground spinning like a big maple tree seed. Had that been a prop from one of the other engines, the outcome could have been different. Number one or number two could have sliced into the fuselage. Number three could have also taken out number four.

One day the C.O. sent an Orderly to tell us they wanted us to deliver a skeleton flight crew to Woodbridge to pick up one of the Group's airplanes. The airplane to be picked up had been forced to land at Woodbridge because of battle damage. Limited repairs, enough to make it airworthy, had been made. It could now be flown back to Horham for further repair and return to combat status.

The flight to Woodbridge was a short one or, in pilot-copilot language, it was just a "Gear up" and "Gear down" distance.

Woodbridge was the main emergency airfield, practically on the shore of the Channel.

Its primary purpose was to provide a place to land badly damaged aircraft after they had been nursed across the Channel. To continue further flight was not only real hazardous, but was asking for far more than Lady Luck could be expected to provide.

The field was just a large square of blacktop —- about a mile square. Most of the planes forced to land there usually were barely under control. Thus, they were unable to be maneuvered to line up with runways. The unwritten rule was, "If you can see the field, come straight in from whatever heading." However, there was a part of the field marked like a runway. It was equipped with FIDO. This is an acronym for "Fog, Intensive Dispersal Of". FIDO was nothing more than a ditch along each side of the runway. When in use, these two ditches were filled with gasoline and ignited. The heat from the flames dispersed the fog near the runway and the light of the fires served as a beacon. It did work and was used. We, however, never had the "pleasure" of using it, for which I had no regret.

After landing we wandered around the field and looked at some of the hulks —- this gave us a much greater appreciation of the durability of the B-17 and other airplanes. Some of them were so badly damaged it seemed unwise to even crawl into them on the ground, let alone be in one in the air.

The Field had been cut out of a pine forest. As we climbed out of the airplane, one of the crew, Larry, I believe, asked if we could take back a Christmas tree. I said neither "yes" or "no". However, I did mention that I would enter and exit the airplane through the front hatch. Thus, if some strange cargo, such as a Christmas tree or two, found its way into the back of the airplane, I, more than likely, would be totally unaware of it. Further, I suggested that if he did leave the airplane, it probably would be a good idea to take the fire axe with him as some unprincipled person might steal it.

So, for the Christmas of 1944 one Enlisted Men's hut and one Officers' hut were decorated with live (recently dead) trees. What could be used to trim the tree? Popcorn and chaff (strips of aluminum foil used to confuse enemy radar) were excellent.

Later we were told we had committed a serious crime in that all of the trees at Woodbridge belonged to the King and there were severe penalties for cutting and/or stealing them. We were never

THE "HOT" CHRISTMAS TREE

LEFT TO RIGHT, BACK; JACK SHEETS AND CHARLIE DYE
FRONT: JIM PURDY, LARRY FRANCESCHINA, AND GEORGE HASSELBACK

caught. This, was in spite of the fact that Base Public Relations types took a photo of the trimmed tree in the enlisted crew quarters and sent copies to their home town papers.

Shortly after the Christmas tree pirating act, the Battle of The Bulge began. We knew that our troops needed our support; however, the weather was awful. We chomped at the bit, while fog, snow, frost and clouds down on the deck kept us sitting on the ground.

Finally, on Christmas Eve the weather cleared and we got back into the air. It was our 15th mission. Our target was an airfield near the front. We were to knock it out in order to deny the Germans aerial support for their troops. We encountered moderate flak and the airplane sustained minor damage.

While this mission was just across the lines, it was one of the longer ones at 8 hours. This, for the reason the route to the target was purposely very tortuous in order to get the Luftwaffe in the air and make them use up their fuel as they guessed as to what our target was.

For this mission the Group put up a total of 61 aircraft. A normal complement for the Group to put in the air was 36. Obviously, any airplane that could get off of the ground and carry bombs was flying that day. Surprisingly, considering the condition of some of the planes in the Group, 60 of the 61 made it to the target with no losses.

Missions 16, 17 and 18 finished out 1944. If the 35 mission tour held up, we were over half way there. These three targets, Koblenz, Kassel and Hamburg were fairly easy for us. For the first time we encountered fighters in considerable numbers at Hamburg.

The 95th lost 2 aircraft and the 100th, "The Bloody Hundredth" flying behind us, lost 12. All told, the 3rd Bomb Division lost 27 aircraft out of the 526 dispatched. Luckily, we came through all three of these missions without a single hole in the airplane.

Charlie's tail gunner's position in the rear of the airplane gave him a ring side seat to the 100th's misfortune on the Hamburg raid. His instructions to me as the fighters hit the 100th were: "LET'S GET THE HELL OUT OF HERE! SIR"

Charlie was never hesitant nor reluctant to give me advice. One day he said to me: "Lieutenant, Sir, do you know that for every foot the nose of this airplane moves on the horizon the tail moves 12 feet?" I guess I had been doing a "tap dance" on the rudder pedals and shaking him up quite a bit. I promised to "watch it" hereafter.

CHAPTER 17
HALF WAY THROUGH
AND
THE NEW COLONEL

The first two missions, numbers 19 and 20, in the new year were both strictly milk runs. Again, no holes in the airplane. This was certainly a situation we could live with and live because of.

The next, the 21st, mission would be unusual. However, before telling that story, some background needs to be laid.

When we came to the 95th, the Group C.O. was a likeable fellow by the name of Colonel Carl Truesdell, Jr. He was a cigar smoking West Pointer and the son of a General. He believed in running a somewhat easy-going but extremely proficient unit. He was strong on having a good operational outfit, but chose to look the other way when it came to some of the Army spit and polish. This latter attitude was best typified by his approach to the dress code for the Saturday night Officers' Club dance.

It was not a complete "let the bars down" situation. Class A's were required; however, the necktie was exempted. The shirt collar could be unbuttoned and laid back over the blouse collar. With some imagination, this could be a college dance with sport shirts and sports jackets.

His tolerance of the men's ignoring certain iron clad rules of the military apparently did not set well with the Wing Staff or with some of the people in the upper echelon.

The following activity probably had nothing to do with the Colonel's departure. In fact, more than likely, the Colonel was unaware there was more or less free access to the base by British female civilians. Most of these visits were in connection with the Saturday night dances. However, there were occasions when some of these "guests" slept over and over and over....

There was one of these ladies who, for a time, called Olson's hut "home". After being there for a time, she decided to relocate to our hut. At that point, Olson suggested it would be both kind to her and practical for her "hut mates" to offer to escort her to the communal bath house for a bath. Acting upon that suggestion, we extended the offer. She accepted, so Olson and I escorted her to the bath house and back. We also stood guard (outside and with no peeking) while the necessary operations were completed.

There were kind souls in the hut who saw to it that food was provided either from the mess hall or packages from home.

After a short stay with us, she decided to move up in the ranks and attempted an invasion of the Squadron C.O.'s hut. However, an overt move on her part one night, while the major was asleep, really grabbed him where it hurt and resulted in her eviction from the base.

I don't know whether there was any connection with this incident, but in December, for some reason or other, Colonel Truesdell was kicked upstairs. Although the motion picture, "Twelve O'clock High", was to come some years later, the Colonel's move had a certain "Twelve O'clock High" flavor to it. However, the 95th's combat performance was without serious or obvious problems, unlike that of the mythical Bomb Group in the movie.

Colonel Truesdell's replacement was a white haired Colonel by the name of Jack Shuck. He, too, was a West Pointer; but, unlike Truesdell, he acted it. That is, "All things military are serious. No time, space or place for deviations from the code exists."

Shortly after he arrived, he flew his first mission as a copilot in a "tail end Charlie" position. In rapid succession he moved up through element lead (copilot) and squadron lead (copilot).

On the 5th of January, 1945, the Colonel was in command of the Group (lead copilot). The target that day was Frankfurt, which was not all that deep into Germany. The Group took off and assembled. However, instead of concentrating on proceeding to get the primary job done, the Good Colonel insisted the Group formation look picture perfect before it took off to join the bomber stream. There was nothing really wrong with that desire; however, his nit-picking resulted in the Group hitting the U.K. departure point a couple of minutes late.

As the Group lead he saw this as no big deal. Just pick up the airspeed a few miles an hour and we would soon catch up. Only one problem —- the rest of the aircraft in the Group were really having to crowd things to keep up at this higher speed.

By now we had moved up to element lead. This meant we did not have quite as hard a time keeping up as did our wing men. However, with the extra power we were having to pull, our rate of fuel consumption began to become a real concern. Even though we were still climbing, I decided to pull the mixtures back to auto lean and told Mac to keep a sharp eye on the engine cylinder head temperatures, but not to open the cowl flaps any wider than "trail". And, to let me know if the indicated temperatures began to move into the red. The cylinder head temperature gauge needles hung near the top of the yellow band. It looked like we could stay with the Group and not run out of fuel.

As we were about to cross the lines, Jack Sheets, the ball turret, who had a good view of the underside of the airplane, called on the intercom and said, "We're losing quite a bit of oil out of number one." About the same time, the oil pressure on that engine began to fluctuate and drop. I told Mac to shut down number one and to feather that engine's propeller. Maybe we could stay in formation on three engines.

No sooner had that decision been made than Jack was back on the intercom again.

"We're now losing oil out of number two." Number two engine oil pressure was beginning to drop, too.

As far as we were concerned, that day, Colonel Shuck was going to have to go to war without us. Leaning out the mixture had caused detonation and blown cylinder head gaskets on number one and two engines. This had happened, in spite of keeping the cylinder head temperature out of the red.

Still, having both our bomb load and a fair amount of fuel aboard, it seemed to be imprudent to feather number two as long as there was some oil pressure and we could continue to pull a bit of power out of it.

We left the formation and started to look for a place to set the bird down. I wasn't sure we could get back to the Channel to get rid of the bombs before we lost number two completely. With two engines out on one side and a full load of bombs, the airplane would not fly very long or very far. Plus, there was the knowledge that number three and four engines had been worked as hard as one and two, and they might also be on the verge of giving up the ghost.

Luckily, we were not too far from an emergency field in the north of France. So, we headed for it —- managed to raise the tower and get numbers and let them know what shape we were in and that we were headed in their direction.

We let down to 1,500 feet AGL, and shortly we picked up the field dead ahead. We began a straight-in final approach. In our condition fooling around flying a by-the-book traffic pattern just didn't make good sense. About the time we hit 1,000 feet, the field "disappeared." With the sun in our eyes, Mac and I "lost" the field in a thick layer of ground haze.

We "found" the runway when we passed over the approach end of it which was about 200 feet below us. There was no way we were going to get on the runway and get stopped before we ran out of the hard stuff. Only thing to do was to "go around". I told Mac to clean up (raise the gear and flaps) the ship as I "firewalled" numbers three and four and inched number two up a little.

I told Mac to keep his eye on the gauges and take as much power as he could out of number two. It was not much, but under the circumstances we needed every little bit of power we could get.

Mac called the tower and told the operator we were going around. The control tower operator informed us the field had a left hand pattern. With two engines out on the left side, it was going to be a right hand pattern for us. Mac told him we were doing a right hand pattern. Now was the time to remember my check ride at Hobbs. DON'T EVER, EVER TURN IN TO TWO DEAD ENGINES!!

As we struggled down the runway clawing to regain a little altitude, we heard on the radio an airplane somewhere behind us ask for landing instructions and traffic information. The tower operator came back to them with the numbers and then added, "the only traffic is a B-17 in a right hand pattern trying to go around on two, but I don't think he's going to make it."

194

Mac and I had our hands full, but we were not too busy to let that comment go unanswered. My transmission went something like this, "You fly your god damned tower and I'll fly this airplane. Don't go away. We'll be back in a few minutes."

And we were. It was a struggle and it took awhile. This time we touched down on the numbers with one of the smoothest landings I think I ever made.

One further problem was to beset us before we got parked. As we crossed a cast iron drainage grate in the taxi way, the right main broke it and the wheel dropped into the drain. Fortunately, the drain was shallow so the props didn't hit the surface of the taxi way. It was apparent, whoever built the airfield had not counted on a heavily loaded B-17 using it. At that point, I decided that this airplane was now someone else's problem. So, we shut things off, asked the tower to send someone to pick us up, grabbed our gear and waited for our ride.

It would take some time to get the airplane out of the drain, get the bombs unloaded and change out the two engines. We would be flown back to the U.K. as soon as transport was available. In the meantime, they put us up in an old Chateau which had been the German General von Runstedt's headquarters. It was named La Petite Challet, as I recall. We were near Laon, France. The evidence of war was all about. In fact, we were told to be on the lookout for German snipers.

I'm not sure whether that was fact or just an attempt by the ground personnel to impress the "flyboys".

We spent four days there before being flown out in the bomb bay of a B-24. That trip in the bomb bay had to go down as one of the more hazardous flights I have taken. I can still smell the gasoline fumes.

When we got back to the base, we found out the full extent of the Colonel's folly. Eight of the 36 Group aircraft turned back early because of either equipment failure or fuel shortage. Nine aircraft, including us, were forced to land on the Continent.

Then, guess what happened? The good Colonel was awarded the Distinguished Flying Cross for "outstanding" leadership under adverse conditions. The final insult was that we had to stand formation while the award was made. Nowhere in the citation was it mentioned that the adverse conditions were of Colonel's own making.

This was not the last from the good Colonel. In order to shape the place up it was decided the sports shirt look at the Saturday night dances had to go. And, unless a mission was scheduled, there would be, of all of the chicken s—t things, a <u>Saturday morning inspection</u>. This included all of the Officers' quarters as well as those of the Enlisted Men.

The word of this decision sent the Nissen hut "attorneys" into action. The <u>Officer's Guide</u> became the most sought after and read book in the house. Finally, after some searching, the desired section was found.

Under the section entitled "Courtesies Rendered by an Officer to His Senior Officer," this paragraph appeared:

> "In an officer's quarters such courtesies are not observed as are prescribed when an officer enters a squad room or tent occupied by one or more enlisted men."

The prescribed courtesies referenced were:

> "Procedure When an Officer Enters a Squad Room or Tent. In a squad room or tent, individuals [enlisted personnel] rise, uncover (if unarmed), and stand at attention when an officer enters. If more than one person is present, the first to perceive the officer calls, 'Attention'."

This meant that when the C.O. came in, we did not have to snap to attention and perform the rest of the military gymnastics. We were prepared for the first inspection.

We were not to be disappointed. On the first Saturday morning set aside for the inspection, the Adjutant popped in the hut door and yelled "Attention". The group stayed put. Those in the sack stayed there and the card players kept their seats but they did pause and look up to see what would happen next. The Adjutant's face had a slightly perplexed look.

The Colonel asked why the beds had not yet been made and the place straightened up. The reply was, "The Orderly hasn't been around yet this morning, Sir." The Colonel and the Adjutant did some harrumping, and commented upon the general pig pen nature of the place and departed the scene. The Adjutant tried to save the day by saying, "As you were, men," as he went out the door. This was a useless bit of instruction as we had not been in any other condition during their brief visit.

We later heard that while inspecting another hut, the Adjutant had attempted to exit through the nailed shut door with the result that he crashed into it and the Colonel, in turn, crashed into him. Their retreat back down the aisle and out the other door was somewhat embarrassing —- in spite of the Adjutant's comments that nailing the door shut was unsafe should a fire occur.

The inspection routine was tried once more before the Colonel recognized this was going to be more of a loser than a winner.

There is just one more Colonel Shuck story. One night Olson, a couple of other fellows, and I were having our usual evening's entertainment at the Club when we got word the Group was to be put on alert for a mission the next day. We quickly rushed to the bar and purchased a half case of beer and took it into the lounge. We had been there for a short time when who shows up but the good Colonel. He eyed the case of beer and said, "My, what a windfall of beer! I think I'll join you." The other two fellows, as they departed, said they had to fly tomorrow and were going to hit the sack. This left Olson, the Colonel and me. The Colonel asked if either of us were flying the next day. We didn't know, but said we were not. We found out later that we were.

Our conversation was wide ranging and more philosophical than anything else. In due course, age became the center topic. After some time, Olson decided to issue his summation. It was, "I think that all people over 45 ought to be shot. That way we would avoid the Hitlers and Mussolinis of the world." I don't know how old the Colonel was, but from his reaction, I expect he was over 45. His red face made a nice contrast with the full head of white hair. He proceeded to lecture Olson about how not all people over 45 were like Hitler, etc. When he ran out of steam, he left. If Olson was shaken or chastened by all this, he sure hid it extremely well.

CHAPTER 18
THE NEW AIRPLANE

Mission 22 was not one of the rougher ones. The flak was accurate and we did manage to pick up a few "ventilation" openings in the airplane. We considered ourselves lucky having escaped with so little damage. However, when we got back the airplane's crew chief was more than a little p——d off at us. This was a brand new airplane and this had been its first mission. We had gone out and gotten holes shot in it!!

Except for two missions, we would fly this same airplane (s/n 43-38826) to the end.

Its call sign was Abush J, Jig". Abush was the call sign for all 412th Squadron airplanes. "Jig" was the phonetic alphabet word for the letter J assigned to this particular aircraft. To complete the picture, when we contacted the 95th's control tower, the call sign was "Bezel".

Although we had snow in December, it had not been heavy nor had it stayed long. But, now, in January, we had snow which stuck around for a while. The base had enough equipment to move the snow from the runways; however, they didn't have enough to clear the taxi ways and hardstands. This situation provided us with a new thrill. That is, taxiing a 60,000 pound airplane on the icy surface.

The least application of brakes would lock up the wheels and the whole mess would go sliding toward that edge of the taxi way which happened to slope downward. There were a few airplanes bent, but we managed to avoid bending any metal ourselves. I'm sure this was due more to luck than skill.

Speaking of snow, on one mission, I forgot whichever one it was, but whatever, snow and a bomb did combine to give us another new thrill and experience. On this particular mission, one of the airplanes in the Group had a bomb fail to drop and hang up in the bomb bay. On the way back they had tried to get rid of it over the Channel, but their efforts were not successful. They decided to put the pins back in the fuses and land with the bomb still hung up. As luck would have it, when the Pilot set the plane down (it must have been hard), the bomb came loose, crashed through the closed bomb bay doors, hit the runway, skidded and spun to a stop in the middle of the main runway near the intersection with the other two (shorter) runways. This closed all three runways and shut down the whole field.

There were still a number of us up in the air. That, in itself, would not have been more than a small inconvenience, except there were snow squalls marching through the area at the time. So, here we, and a dozen or so other planes, were circling the field at about 500 feet waiting for the Ordnance people to remove the bomb. As a snow squall moved in, we would not only lose sight of the field but also of the other planes in the air around us. After what seemed an eternity, the bomb was removed from the runway and we landed.

Subsequent briefings included directions as to what to do in case you had a hung bomb and couldn't get rid of it. That is, stay up in the air and wait until everyone else was on the ground before landing. I knew the pilot of the plane which "bombed" the runway. He was "flakkie" before he saw the first burst of the stuff.

On another mission return, as we neared our base, we saw a lot of smoke and fire at a nearby base. We decided to go take a good low altitude look at it. When we got near and saw what it was, we sure got the hell out of there real quick. One of the 100th Bomb Group's planes had crashed into their bomb dump. It was very, very spectacular. It could only happen to the 100th.

Mission 23 presented us with another new experience. This was to be one of the shorter missions. Dusseldorf was the target. More precisely, the City of Dusseldorf was the target, so we were now, for the most part, trying to disrupt transportation by knocking down the buildings in the center of the city in order to block the streets, roads and railways. This mission's purpose was to take out a railroad yards which also happened to be right in the city center.

We started our takeoff roll with everything appearing to be normal. I waited for Mac to begin calling off the airspeed. However, he sat there like a sphinx. I asked him to give me a reading. He came back with "There isn't any." By now, it was certainly obvious we were moving fast enough that we should be getting an airspeed reading. We also knew we were going too fast and were too far down the runway to attempt to abort the takeoff.

We were going to fly. There was no "or else" about it. We held the plane on the runway to the bitter end and then pulled it off, barely missing the farm house which sat a few hundred yards off the end of the runway. We were flying. Using power settings, the altimeter and the rate-of-climb readings, we proceeded to climb out and join the Group. Given the fact we had a full load of fuel and bombs on board, there was no point trying to land now. Might as well go and dump the bombs on those deserving of them.

The absence of an airspeed indicator would mean we would not be able to do a very good job of leading the element. We could stall out the whole element, including ourselves, if we were not careful. As radio silence was still in effect, it was not possible to use the radio to ask one of the wing men to take over element lead. Finally, after much arm and wing waving, the number 2 man got the idea and took over the lead. We changed places with him and hoped he wouldn't stall us out. If he did, we wouldn't know it until it was about to happen.

The mission was uneventful. It is likely that assessment was the result of our preoccupation with the airspeed indicator problem. On the way home I asked Purdy to see if he could find out what was wrong with the airspeed indicator. He poked around behind the instrument panel and soon found the problem. Apparently, the airspeed indicator had been replaced just before this flight. In reconnecting the replacement, the static and the pitot (pressure) lines had been crossed. Jim switched them around and "Presto" we had our airspeed indicator working. This would and did make the landing much easier. The crew chief and I had a little talk about this matter after we landed. This was not "Abush J, Jig".

At this time I was called into the Squadron C.O.'s office and asked if I would be interested in transferring from combat crew status to Squadron Staff. The Staff position would be as either Assistant Operations Officer or (eventually) Operations Officer.

Squadron and Group formations were led by specially picked Lead Crews. The Operations Officer, serving as the Command Pilot, rode in the Copilot's seat of the lead aircraft. The Lead Crew Copilot flew in the tail gunner's position so he could monitor what was happening to the Squadron or Group. He, then, was responsible for keeping the Command Pilot informed as to what was going on behind the lead plane.

Taking this job would mean leaving the crew. They would either be given another Pilot or broken up and used as replacements on other crews. This was an obvious down side of the offer. The pluses were: have my tour reduced from 35 to 30 missions and be promoted to Captain in about two months. There was another downer, however, it was after some time off (probably home leave) following the 30 missions, I would be expected to fly another 30 missions as Command Pilot.

After mulling things over for awhile, I decided not to take the offer. The deciding factor was that the crew had stuck with me through good and bad times. I felt that if I left them I would, in fact, desert them. I declined the offer.

Mission 24 was a deep penetration to Chemnitz. We picked up some flak as we crossed the front lines, but after that it was a milk run.

On one mission, again I forget which one, we were heading across the Channel just as the sun began to rise. There were a few wispy clouds scattered across the entire height of the sky. The rising sun tinted them a warm, rosy hue. The sun was still low enough so the ground was nothing but dark purple shadows. As we were taking in the scenery, suddenly, from the ground, as if some unseen giant hand had taken a piece of chalk, a white line rapidly rose and trailed off into the pale blue sky above. We had witnessed the launching of a V-2 rocket. Shortly, it was followed by another. The rate at which the exhaust trails were generated confirmed the awesome speed of these rockets.

Speaking of "trails in the sky", we often left our signature in the sky. These lines are more commonly know as contrails. The "con" is an abbreviation for condensation. Among the various gases emitted in the engine exhaust is water vapor. If the air through which the plane is flying is relatively very humid, the additional moisture added to it by the engine exhaust results in the formation of contrails. They are nothing more than miniature man-made ice crystal clouds. We despised seeing them for two reasons. First, the screening effect of the contrails would allow enemy fighters to approach unseen from the rear. Second, from the ground, they clearly indicated our presence and, from our apparent heading, gave a clue as to our intended target.

If you could be objective about them, they were spectacular. And, it was fascinating to watch as adjacent ships spun them.

On February 15, 1945, we were scheduled for the mission to Cottbus for the purpose of destroying the railway yards there. However, we were unable to participate due to the loss of number four engine while en route to the target. We returned to base with our ten 500 pound General Purpose bombs unused.

We had gone far enough (that is, we crossed into enemy held territory) for the abortion to be counted as a mission flown. This meant we now had only 10 missions to go to make the 35. That is, of course, if they didn't raise the "magic" number from 35 to 50. Rumors to that effect were rampant.

Mission number 26 was two days after the Cottbus abort. This time we were sent off to hit Frankfort. The note on the bomb tag for this mission reads: "To Put Rubble in Streets". This we did. There was light flak encountered, but we escaped unscathed.

After a week off we now really started to work. Missions 27 through 30 were flown on consecutive days: the 24, 25th, 26th and 27th of February.

The first of the series was to Bremen. The purpose of the mission was to take out a railroad bridge. This was the first time we carried anything bigger than a 1,000 pound bomb. For this trip we had two 2,000 and two 1,000 pounders on board. When they were released, you could feel the bird give a very noticeable sigh of relief.

The next mission was to Munich. Our first and only trip there. Again, quoting from the bomb tag, our target was "Arms, legs and old ladies." Strategic targets were becoming even more and more scarce. Flak defenses were far from scarce, however. We really got the airplane ventilated.

While under fire, Larry came on the intercom with the words: "I've been hit!". I asked George to check him out. For what seemed like a long time there was no conversation. Then came sounds of laughter. I asked to be let in on the joke, if there was one. Finally, an explanation was forthcoming. A piece of flak had entered the bottom of the airplane near Larry's position. After penetrating the aircraft's skin, the fragment hit the underneath side of the plywood walkway sending a long splinter flying. The sharp end of the splinter hit Larry in the rear. Fortunately, the wound was no bigger than a pin prick. It healed by the time we got back to the base, which thereby, deprived Larry of a Purple Heart.

"Abush J, Jig" took a real licking on this trip and was out of service for the following day so that the many holes could be patched. The crew chief was really unhappy this time. Not particularly because the airplane was new, but because he and his crew would be spending most of the night out in the cold cutting and riveting patches over the many holes.

After the pounding we had taken at Munich, it was a shock at the next morning's briefing to learn that the target for today was "Big B", Berlin. This was a bit much: "Little B", Munich and "Big B", three "bad" targets, in three consecutive days.

The Berlin raid was one of the biggest of the war. All three Air Divisions went there that day. Over 1,100 heavy bombers dropped more than five and three quarters million pounds of bombs on the city. About one third of the bombs were instantaneously fused (exploded on impact); another one third had 4 hour delay fuses and the balance had 8 hour delay fuses. Our 12 bomb load was equally divided between 500 pound General Purpose and Incendiary bombs. All of our bombs were instantaneously fused.

I'm sure all Berlin citizens were echoing General Sherman's comment after that day.

The flak over Berlin was moderate, and we escaped without a hit or a hole.

After three days in a row, we felt sure we would get the next day off. Wrong.

The next morning we were up and at them once more. This time the target was Leipzig. This was another target with the same reputation as those of the preceding three days. Again this was an 8th Air Force maximum effort. Over 1,000 heavies took part. The bomb tonnage dropped on the city by the Eighth Air Force was about the same as that deposited upon Berlin the previous day. Our bomb load was the same as the one for Berlin. Our target was the railway yards which happened, by coincidence, to lie in the city center.

As with Berlin, flak was moderate and "Abush J, Jig" escaped without a hole.

It was now "Five to go!" We were given two days off in preparation for the final push.

Back to work on March 2nd with the target being Dresden. The RAF had pretty well destroyed the city by this time; however, 8th Air Force command apparently thought the rubble needed rearranging. So we did it. Flak was non-existent. We did see a number of enemy fighters, some of which were the Me 262 jets and the Me 163 rockets. Our "Little Friends", the P-51 escorts, kept the jets, rockets and the conventional fighters away from us one more time.

Again, we had back-to-back missions. The next day we were off to Brunswick to take out a tank factory. However, oddly, our bomb load was split between 3,000 pounds of General Purpose bombs and 3,500 pounds of incendiary bombs. This was odd because GP's were used for specific targets such as tank factories, bridges, etc., while incendiaries were used mostly for houses, buildings and other flammable structures. So, Headquarters must have reasoned, "If they don't hit the tank factory, maybe they'll burn the town down." In any event, flak was meager and "Abush J, Jig" was spared any new holes.

CHAPTER 19
THE END IS IN SIGHT

After three days off we were back in the air again. This time on March 7th we were headed to Dortmund to obliterate (hopefully) a benzol plant. The shortness of the mission coupled with the availability of a number of landing strips on the Continent allowed the trading of fuel load for bomb load. This time we had fourteen 500 pounders on board for a total bomb load of 7,000 pounds. Again, the flak was light and we escaped without damage. It looked like we might make it through the whole thirty five.

It was down to just two more to go. Olson and I now had the same number of missions completed. I had closed the gap between us during January and February. It looked like it might be possible for us to finish on the same mission. However, that possibility became less likely when he was scheduled for the March 6th mission and we were not.

We both flew the March 7th mission; his 34th and our 33rd.

We were both scheduled for the March 9th mission to Frankfort. This would be Olson's 35th and our 34th. The "target" was an aircraft components factory. I put target in quotations because I imagine that by this time the factory output was near nil. This suspicion was confirmed by the fact that our bomb load was 1,800 pounds of 100 pound demolition bombs and 5,000 pounds of 400 pound incendiaries. Headquarters must have thought, "There's probably little left to break; so, let's set fire to the rubble." The flak on the way to and at the target was moderate but accurate, and poor "Abush J, Jig" picked up a few more holes.

However, on return to base there was bad news. Olson had gone down on the Continent. From what we could learn, everybody was O.K. It was just a broken airplane. We hoped that to be true.

March 10th arrived; it was the day for our final mission. This time it would be another trip to Dortmund. We'd been there three days before. We almost felt like commuters. As on the three day earlier trip to Dortmund, we were loaded with 7,000 pounds of 500 pound GP's. The target this time was the railroad yards. This was the mission we had been looking forward to some eight months. THE LAST ONE!!

Being young, and convinced we were invincible (Olson's recent experience notwithstanding), we felt some post mission celebration planning was called for. We rounded up two small gunny sacks of Very pistol flares (no extra red-reds) and a second Very pistol. The extra pistol was for Charlie in the tail. All the bottles of booze which had been stashed especially for this day were placed in the ground crew chief's tent at "Abush J, Jig's" hard stand.

The mission was easy but with moderate and accurate flak. However, we were untouched. SOMEONE was obviously looking out for us.

On the return, as we made landfall at the English coast, I received permission to leave the formation and head for the base.

Naturally, this was not going to be a leisurely cruise at 150 mph and 10,000 feet altitude. Instead, we were going down to 1,000 feet and put 200 on the "clock". Not flat out, as now was definitely not the time to break any of the machinery. The 1,000 foot altitude ensured that the flares would be burned out before they hit the ground. As we approached the base, I gave the tower a call and requested landing instructions and permission to "inspect" the runway before landing. The tower was understanding and, as usual, very cooperative.

I passed the word (I thought) to cease firing the Very pistols as we were now going to be close enough to the ground for the flares to still be burning when they hit the ground. The runway was very thoroughly and closely inspected several times followed by an appropriate chandelle at the end of each "inspection". For what some people thought was a stogy old bomber, the B-17 can put on a pretty impressive show at low altitude. Having gotten that out of our system, we landed and taxied to the hard stand.

There, I learned Charlie had either not heard or disregarded the "Cease Very pistol fire" order. He had sent one flare, still burning, into the base fuel dump. Fortunately, there was someone nearby who promptly extinguished the flare by putting a sand bag on it. No harm occurred. For a few moments, however, there had been the possibility of the 95th's fuel dump going up in flames like the 100th's bomb dump we had "inspected" a few months earlier.

We climbed out of the airplane and headed for the crew chief's tent. Who should be there waiting for the party to start? No one but Olson. Apparently he had "leaned" very heavily on the mechanics at the Continent emergency field to get his plane fixed so he could get back for the party.

We stood in a circle inside the tent and proceeded to open the booze, bottle by bottle, and pass it around until all of the bottles were emptied. One of the bottles was a bottle of Southern Comfort which Barbara had sent me. As to the number of bottles we had, I have no recollection. As the celebration went on, things became less clear. When the last "soldier" was dead, we headed to the debriefing room. Lo and behold, the rest of the Group had landed, been debriefed and the place shut down while we were out at the hard stand partying. Because briefing had ended before we got there, I was "unable" to

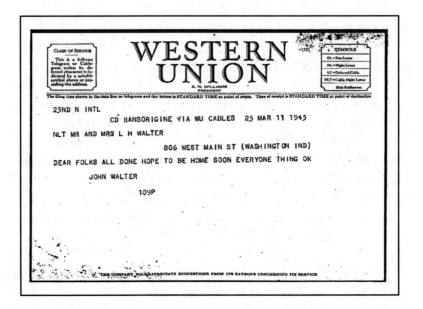

turn in my mission info sheet which is reproduced in APPENDIX. It's the only one I was able to keep.

The celebration continued on into the night. Unfortunately, the celebration turned out to be too much for Charlie. He decided to "borrow" the Colonel's Jeep. As if that weren't bad enough, he ran the thing into a ditch. He was unhurt. However, instead of putting distance between the Jeep and himself, he entered the nearby hanger and either passed out or went to sleep.

Once the Jeep was noticed missing from its last known parking spot, the MP's were hot on the trail. It didn't take them long to find the Jeep and Charlie and put two and two together and reach the right conclusion.

Charlie was confined to base pending courts martial. He was taken off of the orders to return to the Z. of I. (Militaryese for the Zone of the Interior. In plain English, The States.)

Unfortunately, Charlie was selected to be an example of what can happen when you screw up. By the time he came to trial, I had left the Base and he literally had no one to speak on his behalf. The result was he had the book thrown at him. He did not get to come home until the Group was deactivated and transferred back to the States. He was reduced in rank from a Staff Sergeant to a buck private and heavily fined.

This was the last mission for John Ingleman, Jack Sheets, Larry Franceschina, Charlie Dye and me. Jim Purdy, George Hasselback and Bob McCoy would finish soon after.

When the partying had subsided, I managed to get off cablegrams to the folks and Barbara telling them my tour was finished, and I expected to be home soon.

The next day, in spite of a hangover, it felt as if a big load had been taken off our backs. It was hard to realize WE HAD MADE IT THROUGH!! While not expressed out loud, I'm sure all of us wished Tom and Nelson were there to share in our relief.

During the war this phrase was often used: "There are no Atheists in a fox hole." From a personal standpoint, I can vouch: "There are no Atheists in the cockpit." On ever mission, unspoken words were said to One who was with us but could not be seen.

It had taken us eight months to get in our 35 missions. During that same time the Group had flown 60 missions. Because of leave given after the loss of Tom and Nelson, we missed the opportunity to fly for two weeks. For another two weeks the 95th didn't fly any missions. Those were times when the weather was just too lousy to put airplanes in the air.

There were periods when we flew often.

On five occasions, we flew missions on two successive days. On one occasion we flew three days in a row, and one time we flew four days in a row. This latter was for our 27th through 30th missions.

Now, for us, the War was put on hold. We had absolutely nothing to do. We just sat around waiting for those orders which would send us to the Zone of the Interior, and good old U.S.A. After a few days of the inactivity and boredom, Olson and I took off for one last look at London.

CHAPTER 20
ON THE WAY HOME

A few days later we returned to the base and learned that our orders had been issued; we needed to check in our combat gear, get our stuff packed and be ready to move out within a very few hours.

We had not given much thought as to how we would be sent back to the U.S. Probably by air, we assumed. Turned out to be a very wrong assumption. We were ordered to proceed to Southampton and await transport by ship.

Well, while not as good as flying home, we figured that we'd be sent on one of the "Queens" and race across the Atlantic in about 5 days. We most certainly wouldn't be sent home by troop ship in a convoy!!!

While waiting for our embarkation, our stay in Southampton was one continual party. Ingleman became the star of the show. While at the 95th, John had not partied much. But, at Southampton it was different. Perhaps it was the realization that he had survived the 35 missions without a scratch. It might possibly have been the influence of Olson and others, me included.

There were two memorable occasions which featured Lt. John Ingleman.

The first one. John had a small blonde mustache. One night after several drinks, we decided to go in search of some fish and chips. John was in the lead when we came to the door of the fish shop. He had a short cigarette in his mouth. As he was about to open the door, someone decided to leave the establishment. When they did so, they gave the door a mighty outward push. His reflexes being somewhat slowed, John was unable to catch the door to keep it from hitting him in the face. The resulting contact pushed the lit end of the cigarette into the middle of his mustache. The smell of burning hair quickly overpowered the smell of cooking fish for all of us. And for some time, John could only smell burned hair. The next day John was more then a little upset about the hole in the middle of his mustache. He frequently checked to see if his mustache was repairing itself. He didn't want to go home and explain how he got a hole in the middle of his mustache.

The other occasion. Again after a few drinks, we exited a club which had a long stairway leading from the entrance down to the street level. Somehow John stumbled at the top and tumbled down to the street. He was relaxed enough so he was unscathed. However, that little happening did put the very descriptive phrase, "End over end, like a foot locker," into Olson's and my vocabularies. John executed that maneuver with great style and grace.

After a few days of partying, we were herded down to the docks and up the gang plank, to our horror, to board a troop ship!! It was certainly going to be a slow boat to the U.S. It was a "General" class troop ship, a ship which had been especially built for the purpose of hauling troops. I do not recall the name of the ship, except that it was the "General so-and-so".

There were a bunch of us on board: Army Air Force as well as Army ground personnel; both officers and enlisted men.

Neither the officers and enlisted men nor the service branches intermixed in the quarters. Our quarters were, to no one's surprise, below decks and consisted of one hammock in a three high stack. And the room was full of three high stacks with very little aisle space.

We were informed that due to limited supplies there would be only two meals a day. We did find out later the ship's company was eating at least three times a day. This definitely was no way to reduce inter service friction.

We sailed in the dark so it was not until daylight that we found we were part of a convoy. Someone ferreted out the fact that, because we were in a convoy, our little "pleasure" cruise would probably extend for two weeks. There would be plenty of time for John's mustache to recover.

The seas had not yet been cleared of all enemy submarines. We had numerous discussions during the days about how really s——y it would be for us to have survived the Luftwaffe pilots and the German Army antiaircraft gunners 35 times, only to "buy the farm" at the hands of the German Navy.

Fortunately, we took the southern route (near the Azores) and the weather was good. We spent the days sitting on the decks enjoying the sunshine and the warm temperature. A small group of ex-95th types gathered daily to rehash the war and swap stories. Among the group was Greg L'Ecuyer, a 95th and 412th pilot.

Greg was from northern Vermont and came fully outfitted with an Easterner's dry humor. While at the 95th, his wife had sent him a sweater which she had knitted. To say it was too big was an understatement. The bottom of the Vee neck terminated just above his navel. The sleeves began at mid upper arm. The ends of the sleeves came almost to his knees, as did the bottom of the sweater itself. Greg's comment, as he surveyed the fit of the sweater, was, "I'm afraid she's going to be disappointed when she sees that I'm not the man she thought I was."

LT. GREG L'ECUYER And "THE SWEATER"

One day as we sat on the deck chewing the fat we were joined by several ground type Army officers. They were curious about how it was "up there". They were not to be disappointed. When it became Greg's turn, he concluded by saying, "It was tough up there, but it was not near as bad as the trips to Murmansk."

He then began to spin a tale about how before joining the Cadets he had been in the Merchant Marine and pulled convoy duty on the runs to Murmansk. We 95th'ers knew this to be pure fabrication.

However, we didn't expose him. In fact, we compounded the felony by asking all sorts of leading questions, such as: "What does a torpedo look like when it's coming toward you?" and "Did the Me-109's really attack at masthead height?" I'm sure the visitors spread Greg's story around the entire ship. It was a good story even if it was only that, a story, pure fiction.

As we neared the eastern coast of the U.S. we ran into a couple of days of rough weather. Strangely, about the only people who didn't get seasick were Air Force flying personnel. Even the ship's crew got seasick. Greg said the reason for that was the fact they were Coast Guard personnel. As such, until this trip, they had only sailed up and down the Hudson River. Thus, he decided to name them the "Pallisades Vikings". There was also the comment, "Serves 'em right for eating three meals a day."

A few days out, the ship's Captain informed us over the P.A. that President Roosevelt had just died and Harry Truman was now President. About this time, late in the afternoon, we heard explosions just over the horizon. We were told to put on our life jackets and stand by as a submarine had been spotted near the convoy. This renewed our fears of "buying the farm" at the hands of the German Navy. Thankfully, nothing further happened; so we relaxed.

We docked in New York and prepared for the shake down inspection they had warned us about in the U.K. This fear had been used to get us to turn in such combat items as our 45's, binoculars, etc. when we checked out of the 95th. We were told if we were caught with any of this stuff it would be real rough. It turned out that there was no inspection. If it would have fit in our bags, we could have brought back a B-17 with nary a question or comment.

They loaded us aboard a train for a short trip to Camp Kilmer, NJ. It was warm enough for the train windows to be open. So hanging out all of the windows were all kinds of military types yelling and waving at the civilians lining the tracks. It was hard to tell who was making the most noise.

After a short stay at Camp Kilmer, it was on the train again for Camp Atterbury, IN. There I would receive orders for home leave and my next assignment.

Processing at Atterbury was quick, and soon I was now ready to leave for the final leg of the trip home. My orders gave me 21 days of leave. I was to report on May 17, 1945 at Santa Ana, CA for my next assignment. The wheel had come full circle. Santa Ana was the place it all had started more than two years earlier. Now, I was going back.

Even though Camp Atterbury was only about 100 miles from home, it looked like it would take a day, at least, to work out train connections to get me there. But my luck held. There was an officer from Vincennes getting ready to leave at the same time I was. His wife had driven from Vincennes to pick him up. Washington was on their way home. I had a ride.

I arrived home about 9:30 P.M. The folks had been expecting me; however, the exact day and time of arrival had been indefinite. We didn't go to bed until very late that night.

CHAPTER 21
HOME LEAVE AND OTHER THINGS

I spent the next few days sleeping late and enjoying my old bed. I also ate to excess. Even with rationing, Mother was able to create an overflowing abundance at every meal.

Being a "War Hero" I was asked to speak at a War Bond rally at the Baltimore & Ohio railroad shops and at the local Rotary Club.

Barbara and I had corresponded during my stay in England. Our relationship had grown into something more than our being just high school classmates. I decided to take a few days and visit her in Chicago.

During the Chicago visit we decided we would like to make the arrangement permanent. Due to the uncertainty surrounding my next assignment, the date to "tie the knot" was the only thing left unsettled. There was also another occurrence, although of lesser importance, while I was in Chicago —- V-E. (Victory in Europe) day was declared. At least one part of the war was over.

I returned to Washington for a few more days, then left for Santa Ana.

While overseas, Olson and I had both thought it would be great to go into B-29's once we returned to the U.S. However, when I was interviewed at Santa Ana and was asked for assignment preference, without hesitation, I replied: "Air Transport Command".

Plans that had been made in Chicago overcame the lure of B-29's. Olson also had changed his mind; I found this out later when I caught up with him in Long Beach.

As Daugherty Field (also Long Beach Municipal Airport and Long Beach Army Air Base) had an ATC unit stationed there, I requested assignment to that unit. To my surprise, it was granted. So, my next change of station involved a very short trip.

After reporting to Long Beach Army Air Base, one day, while I was in the PX, who should I run into but my Basic Flight Instructor, "Red" Donoghue. At Lancaster he had been a civilian. Some where along the line he had joined up. He was now a Flight Officer. Since I out ranked him, I used the opportunity to give a good natured "going over". We had a good visit. It all seemed to be rather ironic. Here was one of the people who had taught me to fly and earn my commission. In spite of that, he was not granted a commission and was able to wear only Service Pilot wings.

There was a lot to do. However, in order to keep up our skills, we got to fly B-17's, C-47's and C-54's. And, in the process, to qualify for flight pay which was equally, if not more, important!! I was checked out in the C-54 and became involved in ferrying them from Hamilton Field, CA to Long Beach.

Olson and I had reestablished contact. As a result, I had the privilege and honor to serve as his best man when he and Mary Horton were married.

It appeared that I would not be sent very soon, if ever, to war in the Pacific. Also, the Long Beach assignment looked like it might have some permanence to it. Enough so, that Barbara and I could make plans.

THE AUTHOR, MARY HORTON OLSON, HERB OLSON

We settled on July 3rd. Now all I had to do was to find a place for us to live, obtain a leave and get back to Washington on time.

It turned out the difficulty of each step would escalate in the order just listed.

For living accommodations, the best I could do was to find a room with kitchen privileges in the home of two sisters, Marge and Norm(a). Oh yes, John and Betty Roberts, a Navy couple, also had a room there. A cozy arrangement for a house with two bedrooms and two baths. Marge and Norm used the former den as a bedroom. The Roberts and we shared a bathroom which was located between our respective bedrooms. Of course, the kitchen was shared by all. They were all nice people; the place was clean and close to the airport. I made the deal. What helped in my negotiations was the fact that I reminded Marge of her son, a pilot, who had been killed in action. Marge's husband, deceased, had been City Manager of Long Beach. Norma, single, was a good friend of the movie actress, Mae West. She frequently went to visit her in Hollywood.

The next hurdle was to get leave. This turned out to be somewhat difficult as I had just gotten off a 21 day leave the middle of May. The best I could wrangle was 7 days.

Since train travel from Long Beach to Washington took at least 3 days each way, it was obvious I had to get back to Washington in some other fashion. Not having commercial airlines priority, I realized that the only way I could make it was to hitchhike on ATC flights. I left in the evening of June 30 and got to Oklahoma City the next day with little problem. At that point I began looking for a flight to get me to some place near home such as Louisville, St. Louis, Indianapolis, etc. There was nothing. Time began to put the squeeze on me. Finally, I found a flight to Memphis. One more time, my knowledge of railroads came in handy. From Memphis, perhaps I could catch an Illinois Central train north to where it crossed the B&O, change trains there and make it on home. After checking schedules at the Memphis railroad station, I found that a combination couldn't be put together to allow me to be present at my own wedding.

I was really in a time jam, now. It was the afternoon of July 2, the bridal party dinner was that evening, I hadn't gotten my blood test nor the marriage license and I was still in Memphis, more than 300 miles away. The last resort was the bus. I checked with the bus station and found I could get to Evansville early the next morning. EXCEPT!! There was a good possibility of a drivers' strike sometime that night.

I called the folks and asked Dad if he could meet me in Evansville the next morning. This he could do. I got a seat on the bus right behind the driver and for the rest of the night I kept my eyes open for any sign of a picket. At all of the many stops the bus made through out the night, I tensed up expecting a picket to emerge from the shadows and "Shut the operation down." Lady Luck smiled —- there were no unscheduled stops. Dad and Barbara's father met me in Evansville, as planned.

The festivities came off without a hitch —- although the groom had missed the rehearsal the previous evening. John Ingleman came over from Rantoul to serve as the Best Man. After the reception, Barbara and I left for a short honeymoon trip to the resort hotel at French Lick, IN.

(Since it was now probably universally known, I might as well chronicle it here. For two days, while immersed in the process of finding transport home, I had gotten little or no sleep. However, I had no trouble falling asleep the night of July 3, 1945.)

Due to the shortness of my leave, it would be necessary for us to start back on the 5th. That was the situation until Barbara's mother, May, went into action. She was the Executive Director of the local Red Cross office throughout the war; therefore, she knew the right way to go about getting extensions to military leaves. Early on the morning of July 4 the phone rang in our hotel room. It was May, not checking on her daughter's welfare (I don't think), but to say she had obtained a leave extension.

We managed to get Pullman reservations, an upper berth for two. Cozy, but I sure didn't mind. I'm afraid the two older women in the berth below us, who knew we were newlyweds didn't get much sleep. Why, I'll leave to your imagination. You're Wrong!

We settled in at 1927 Atlantic Avenue, Long Beach, CA upon return from Washington. I went back to aviating. This was certainly a change. No sleeping in a barracks. And taking a bus to "work".

I also got a pay raise. I was being paid now the grand total of $379.50/month made up of Base Pay: $175.00; Flying Pay: $87.50; Rental Allowance: $75.00; and Subsistence: $42.00. Not too shabby for 1945 with price controls and rationing in effect. Oh, yes, there were no income tax or social security deductions from the $379.50.

By the middle of August the War was over. After being blasted by two atomic bombs, the Japs got smart and quit. I was now in the peace time Army. This change in status brought no immediate changes.

In the latter part of August, unexpectedly, I was given orders to proceed to Homestead Army Air Force Base in Florida reporting there the first of September for Airline Pilot training. Wives were not authorized to accompany their husbands. It was a six week school which was to qualify us as a First Pilot in C-54's. As a result of the War, the Air Force, via the Air Transport Command, had become a globe girdling airline. This seemed to be a good skill to have now the war was over. Perhaps it would result in a job with a commercial airline. Big problem — leaving my wife of less than two months for six weeks. But after all, I was in the Army, and I had to go where they sent me. No questions asked.

As with all Army flying schools the initial portion of the training was ground school. Homestead was no exception. In this case it was 3 weeks ground school and 3 weeks flying. It was an intensive operation —- seven days a week from 0800 to 2200 (8:00 a.m. to 11:00 p.m.).

The war had officially ended several weeks before; however, the organizational momentum within the Army kept the throttle open when it came to training new C-54 pilots. Then, in early September, reality came upon the scene and school was cut back to 6 days a week with a shorter day, 0800 to 2000. This meant that my stay was going to be longer than the original 6 weeks.

Around the middle of the month a hurricane headed in the direction of Homestead. The buildings on the base were temporary and not, by any stretch of the imagination, were they hurricane resistant. We were given the option of either staying at the base or evacuation to the basement of the local high school or to find shelter on our own.

My room mate, Jack Hubbard, and I took off and hitch hiked to Miami Beach. Jack knew some people in the Roney Plaza Hotel so it was only natural we head there. We got to the hotel just as the hurricane began to get serious. Palm fronds, coconuts and whole palm trees were beginning to fly through the air as we went in the front door. In spite of a lack of electricity and running water, we deemed our stay to be better than being in the basement of a school building.

CHAPTER 22
THE END

After the hurricane had passed, we returned to the base only to find that parts of it had been severely damaged. Those in command were uncertain when repairs would be made and operations resumed. While we students marked time in the storm damaged living facilities, the base operations staff could give no assurance if or when training would restart. This uncertainty dragged on for a couple of weeks. Finally, we were told that ground school would begin the following week and completion now would be the first of November. Then, flight training would start with completion by December 1, 1945.

That did it. I had come there with the understanding that this would be a six weeks course. It now looked like it would be at least three months before I was finished, if then. I had enough points (credits) to enable me to request a discharge. So, I told them I wanted out. They accommodated me. Early in October I was on my way back to Long Beach. The return to Long Beach was by train, through Chicago! We had come to Homestead by commercial air. With Military priority, we had enjoyed the "pleasure" of "bumping" civilians both at the Burbank and again at Nashville, where we changed planes.

Back at Long Beach there was more evidence the Army was changing from war time to peace time operation. A lot of the protocol (chicken s—t) which had been shelved during the war was being taken from the shelf, dusted off and reissued.

Reinforcing my decision to get out of the Service was a particular incident. This was the case of a Colonel who was being sent overseas. I was approached by an officer who asked for a $5.00 contribution for a party for said Colonel. As I did not know this Colonel, I respectfully declined to contribute. The soliciting officer said, "Your name will not be on the posted list of contributors." I knew right then and there, my attitude was wrong. And the chances for it improving were not too great.

I had enough "points" (credits) to be granted a discharge. I decided to do it. Barbara and I had talked it over. The "G.I. Bill" had been passed. This paid tuition and a monthly allotment ($105.00) for ex-military people while they attended college. Barbara would go back to work to make up the cash short fall, and I would go to school and get the Engineering degree which I had abandoned several years before.

Going back to school was not the only option considered when I made the decision to get out of the Air Force. Another option was to apply for a job in what promised to be a growing industry, the airlines. I had multi-engine flight time and rating and some airline pilot training. Of course, there was an overabundance of pilots available for the airlines to choose from. I made some inquiries. The hottest prospect was Eastern Airlines. The best they had to offer, however, was a start as a Navigator on their Caribbean and South America routes. In time, you would work your way up through the engineer's seat, the right seat and finally into the left seat. How long would it take? Anybody's guess. This uncertainly was one factor against that choice. The other was the thought that if a health problem arose, be it eyes, heart or hearing, I could find myself unemployed with few skills to fall back upon. The third reason not to take that route was the pay. It was much less than I was currently receiving as a 1st Lieutenant.

Another option was to join Olson in his business of the importation and sale of mahogany articles made in Central America. That option didn't take long to assess and reject. I liked Olson, but the thought of peddling pieces of wood crafted by Central Americans just was not my "cup of tea".

While waiting to be discharged, I continued to fly. Since my separation orders could come through at any time, however, my flying was limited to ferrying "war weary" C-54's from Hamilton Field (San Francisco) to Long Beach. We took ATC's regular passenger flights (C-47's) from Long Beach to Hamilton Field. There, we (Pilot, Copilot and Flight Engineer) would pickup a C-54 and fly it to Long Beach. We would go up in the morning and back in the afternoon or evening.

In the process, we got some real "junkers". They had been flown by some very brave people on the trans-Pacific Air Transport Command runs. The "relics" were being replaced with newer aircraft. Two of these ferry flights are memorable.

Usually, for any given power setting, the throttles on a C-54 are pretty much lined up in a row. On one airplane there were three different engine models installed. When the power settings were equalized, the throttles were all over the quadrant.

On another night, after we had taken off from Hamilton, I signaled the Copilot to pull up the gear. The landing gear position indicator lights went out, but the landing gear stayed down. We recycled the switch several times, but nothing happened. The Engineer checked fuses and things but found nothing wrong. The three of us talked it over. The choices. One: Return to Hamilton Field and land there. Two: Fly on to Long Beach. We took the second choice. If we were to make a mess on landing, it would be better to make it closer to our homes.

With all the hardware hanging out in the breeze, the airplane was not very quick. To save time and fuel, we decided, rather than climb to get over the mountains, to swing out through the Golden Gate and fly just off of the coast over water. On that route, only one or two thousand feet of altitude would be more than enough. As we headed out through the Golden Gate, we toyed with the idea of flying under the bridge, but decided that was not a real good idea. So, we didn't.

On arrival at Long Beach we called the tower and advised them of our problem. They had some suggestions, all of which we had tried before. But we tried them again to no avail. It was night, thus it was not possible to make a low, slow pass and have someone on the ground check things with binoculars.

They asked us to circle the field so there would be time for the fire and crash trucks to get out to the runway.

We made a slow as possible approach and an easy touch down. And used the brakes with the softest touch possible. Things held. We turned off the end of the runway and stopped. Mechanics were there to run out and put the safety pins in the gear. Apparently, the gear had started up but traveled just enough to turn off the indicator lights.

The gear had then stopped. In our fiddling around, the gear had gone back to full down and locked, but the indicator lights had stayed out. Never found out what was wrong.

On November 1, 1945, the orders came through directing me to San Bernardino Army Air Field, CA for discharge.

On November 18, 1945, three years and three months to the day, after it all started, My War was over.

- O -

During that time, on many occasions, I had experienced fun, joy, apprehension, concern, tragedy, fear, love and regrets.

Foremost in my recall of experiences are the sights and feelings of those experiences some of which I have tried to relate here. I know of no way to adequately describe the sounds and smells which accompanied those experiences. Among those many sensory experiences, there are some sounds and smells which even some 60 years later, I can easily recall and vividly re-experience.

Among the remembered sounds are: cadence counting ("one, two - three, four") as we Cadets marched; the whine of the inertia wheel of a "big round" engine starter; the simultaneous gasp of the crews as the mission briefing target map was uncovered; the muffled explosions of the individual cylinders as a big round engine started and then settled into a uniform beat; the lonely, haunting sound of taps; the start of a new day as announced by the reveille bugler and the nervous chatter of the mission debriefing.

Among the smells recalled are: the clear, crisp, early morning air surrounding the flight line during training; the pungent and almost intoxicating odor of the engine exhaust; the smell of hot engine oil; the damp clamminess of our hut in England; the rankness of the latrines at the 95th; and the acrid, coal smoke saturated air of the Salt Lake City and Lincoln air bases.

Undoubtedly, there are some who view three plus years spent in the Army as a sacrifice. I don't. For me, it was an inconvenience and a career detour and a chance to help.

A sacrifice is what Bill Noland, Tom Sevald, Nelson Kurz and thousands more did.

It was an experience I would not sell, if it was possible.

Nor, would I do it again for any amount of money.

EPILOGUE

Once out of the service, my attention was turned to completing the education which had been interrupted more than three years earlier. In the course of this pursuit I slowly lost touch with my crew members and friends made during the time in service.

Even as we went our separate ways, it took longer to lose contact with Mary and Herb Olson, H.B. Thomas and Larry Franceschina. We saw Herb and Mary occasionally. On one of these times, early in 1946, happened to be when we were considering a trip back to Washington to visit our parents. Our travel problem was created because we didn't own an automobile, and train and airplane tickets were very expensive. At that point, Herb came to the "rescue" by declaring that the best way for us to make that trip was to purchase a surplus BT-13, get it licensed and fly back. Obviously, this had to be a good deal, since he already was the proud owner of a BT-13. I was easily convinced, since a surplus airworthy BT-13 could be had at Dos Palos for the sum of $450.00.

So, that summer with our BT-13's, Herb and I treated the citizens of the fair city of Washington, Indiana to some "spectacular" aerial demonstrations. And a lot of noise.

This was one of the last meetings with the Olsons. We continued to exchange Christmas cards and occasional notes with them into the late 50's. My last contact was while we were living in Scotland and Herb called me from Paris. He had rejoined the Air Force and was on temporary duty in Paris. This was in either 1958 or 1959.

H.B. had gone back to school, also to USC. I occasionally saw him on campus.

After we sold the airplane, in early 1947, and got a car, Barbara and I took a vacation trip up the coast to the area north of San Francisco. We stopped by to see Larry. The visit resulted in a memorable luncheon prepared by his father —- a repast which left no doubt in our minds that he had owned an Italian restaurant in San Francisco.

I graduated from USC in 1949 and we moved to Columbus, Indiana where I joined Cummins Engine Company as a Senior Draftsman. In 1951 our son, Gary was born.

Over the ensuing years, we lost contact with the Olsons, H.B., Larry and the others.

In 1985, I heard of a big 8th Air Force reunion being held in Seattle, Washington. In addition to individual Group reunions, Boeing Aircraft Co. was hosting a 50th Birthday Party for the B-17. I had to go. Am I ever glad I did. For whom should I meet, but H.B. Thomas and Dave Webber.

Dave lived in the Seattle area, so, after the reunion, Dave, H.B. and I took a couple of days to get up-to-date on the events of the preceding 40 years. We lost Dave in December 2000. H.B. and I are still in contact, usually at the 95th reunions.

In 1987 the 95th Bomb Group held its reunion in Colorado Springs. Barbara and I both went. There we ran into Jack Sheets and Charlie Dye. This, of course, served to kick off a very serious effort to locate the rest of the crew. Eventually, we found Larry, Jim Purdy and George (who now preferred to called Bob) Hasselback.

THE BT-13

Ultimately, we were to learn that John Ingleman and Bob McCoy both had passed away sometime earlier. In the searching for John and Bob McCoy I found that Herb Olson had passed away, too, in 1970.

In May 1993 I again had an opportunity to fly a B-17. A good friend, Mike Bealmer, arranged for me to fly from Burlington, Iowa to Columbus in the Commemorative Air Force's B-17, "Sentimental Journey". It was truly a sentimental journey. The Pilot in Command, Colonel Bill Bahle, let me have some stick time. As they say about riding a bicycle, "You never forget how." However, after a long layoff you are somewhat wobbly. I found the same is true of flying.

In 1999 Barbara passed away. In 2000 Ruth Braswell, a long time friend of ours and I were married.

For quite a few years now I have been active, as a volunteer, in the Atterbury-Bakalar Air Museum in Columbus. The museum is located at what is now the Columbus Municipal Airport. The airport was built in 1942 as the Atterbury Army Air Force Base. Among the many features of the Museum is a collection of 1:8 scale model aircraft. These were built by a team consisting of Charles Abbott, Glenn Grube and Joe Grube. One of these models is a B-17G painted in the markings of the aircraft I flew in the latter part of my tour. A photograph of this model is reproduced on the cover of this book. I thank the management of the Museum for allowing the use of this photo. A "visit" to the Museum can be made by connecting to <u>atterburybakalarairmuseum.org</u>

In September 2003, Gary and I participated in a tour of the East Anglia wartime air fields and other sites of World War II interest. Very fortunately, one of the sites visited was Horham. It wasn't surprising to find that the intervening 59 years had wrought considerable changes. However, the one thing that has not changed is the friendliness of the people and their appreciation for what the U.S. did for their Country when it was threatened by Hitler.

This friendliness and appreciation is further expressed in bricks and mortar as a dedicated and hard-working group go about the restoration of the NCO (a.k.a. Red Feather) Club. Among the many we met, were our guides, Frank Sherman and Joan Roper.

One of the other places visited was the base of the 390th Bomb Group. In reading the exhibit material in the control tower museum, I found the answer, albeit an unwanted one, to a question that Dave, H.B. and I had asked each other on a number of occasions. That is, "Whatever happened to Gene Peterson?" (He is the fellow on the left in the photo on page 92.) The answer: He was killed in the November 30, 1944 raid on Merseburg when the lead aircraft, after being hit by antiaircraft fire, went out of control and collided with Gene's plane.

During the war, the use of cameras, when not prohibited, was strongly discouraged. This stance was adopted because of the need to keep the details of the U.S. military activities from enemy hands. As a result, what few pictures I have are not all that good. This also resulted in not having a photograph of Tom Sevald. In fact, the only group photographs of the crew I have were taken after Tom was killed.

Through the courtesy of the Royal Oak (MI) <u>THE DAILY TRIBUNE</u> and the Royal Oak Public Library I obtained the following photograph.

LT. THOMAS F. SEVALD, COPILOT

So now, of the ten members of Crew # 5442 who, almost 60 years ago, left Dyersburg, Tennessee to enter combat the score is:

Killed in Combat
Tom Sevald and Nelson Kurz

Passed Away
John Ingleman, Bob Hasselback
and Charlie Dye

Whereabouts Unknown
Jim McCue and Jack Sheets

Alive and Still Kicking
Larry Franceschina, Jim Purdy and Me

Now, Larry, H.B. and I although separated by half of a continent, are still in touch either by telephone, mail, an occasional visit or at a 95th Bomb Group (H) reunion.

'Nuf said.

APPENDIX

One of the important "tools of the trade" for the pilot of an 8th Air Force heavy bomber was the Pilot Information Sheet. It was a legal sized sheet of paper, printed on both sides, containing a wealth of information about the day's mission. The date and target were omitted in case this sheet fell into the enemy's hands.

The only one of these sheets I managed to keep was for our last mission. The front side is shown on page 239 with an explanation of the contents on the facing page. The back side of the sheets is shown on page 240 with an explanation on the facing page.

Following that are reproductions of the bomb tags upon which I made notes concerning each mission. The tags were only 1-3/8" wide and 2-3/4" long, not a great deal of room for writing. This information is on each tag.

TARGET - City name, usually.
DATE -
BOMB LOAD - Number, size and kind.
DURATION - From take off to landing.
NOTABLE OCCURRENCES -
SPECIFIC TARGET - In parenthesis

EXPLANATION - PILOT'S INFORMATION SHEET >>>>

- FORMATION POSITION IS INDICATED BY THE LAST NAME OF THE AIRCRAFT PILOT. UNDERNEATH THE NAME IS THE LAST FOUR DIGITS OF THE AIRCRAFT SERIAL NUMBER. FOLLOWING THAT ARE THE SQUADRON AND THE INDIVIDUAL AIRCRAFT IDENTIFYING LETTERS, e.g. A - J.

- ON THIS MISSION, THE 95TH IS NOT ABLE TO PUT UP A COMPLETE GROUP (48) AIRPLANES SO 6 ARE "BORROWED", WITH THEIR CREWS, FROM THE 100TH.

- DURING ASSEMBLY, TO IDENTIFY THE SQUADRON, THE LEADER FIRES VERY PISTOL FLARES. MY SQUADRON LEADER (FIREBALL BAKER) FIRED A RED-RED.

- ON THIS MISSION, THE 100TH IS LEADING THE 13TH COMBAT WING FOLLOWED BY THE 95TH AND THE 390TH.

- RADIO MONITORING DUTIES ARE ASSIGNED TO SOME AIRCRAFT. CHANNEL "A" (VHF RADIO) IS USED BETWEEN 95TH A/C. "B" IS USED BETWEEN 13TH COMBAT WING A/C. CHANNEL "C" (A TYPO - SHOULD BE "D") IS OUR CONTACT WITH THE 66TH FIGHTER WING, OUR P-51 ESCORT. COMMAND #2 AND M/F D/F CHANNELS ARE OUR LONG WAVE (SIMILAR TO TODAY'S AM RADIO) FREQUENCIES. AIRCRAFT ASSIGNED CONTROL POINT AND STRIKE MESSAGE DUTIES NOTIFY OUR HOME BASE AS WE PASS THE CONTROL POINTS AND DROP OUR BOMBS.

- FOR THIS MISSION WE WERE PROBABLY WAKENED ABOUT 5:00 A.M. WE DRESSED, HAD BREAKFAST, ATTENDED BRIEFING, AND DREW SPECIAL EQUIPMENT (HEATED SUIT, GLOVES, BOOTS, OXYGEN MASK, PARACHUTE, FLAK HELMET AND FLAK SUIT). WE ARRIVED OUT BY OUR AIRPLANE AT 7:35 A.M. WE STOWED OUR GEAR AND PRE-FLIGHTED THE AIRPLANE AND BY 8:35 WE WERE ON BOARD WITH CHECKLISTS COMPLETED AND READY TO START ENGINES. AT 8:35 WE STARTED ENGINES. WITH ENGINES STARTED AND CHECKED OUT, WE STARTED TO TAXI AT 8:50. DEPARTURE FROM THE HARDSTAND WAS TIMED SO WE WERE IN PROPER TAKE OFF SEQUENCE.

- THE THREE SQUADRON LEADERS TAKE OFF EARLY IN ORDER TO BE IN PLACE WHEN THE REST OF THE SQUADRON REACHES ASSEMBLY ALTITUDE. AS THEY HAVE TO CLIMB TO THE HIGHER ALTITUDE, "B" SQUADRON TAKES OFF FIRST FOLLOWED BY "A" AND THEN BY "C".

- AS WE WERE IN "A" SQUADRON, WE CLIMBED TO 17,999 FEET REACHING THERE AT 10:30. ONCE THERE WE MOVED INTO OUR LOCATION IN THE FORMATION.

- (THE FOLLOWING INFORMATION I PENCILED ON THE ORIGINAL SHEET)
1110 DEPART ENGLISH COAST
1148 CROSS EUROPEAN COAST AND PICK UP FIGHTER ESCORT
1213 START BOMB RUN
1224 DROP BOMBS
1230 REACH RALLY POINT
1300 CROSS FRONT LINES
1419 CROSS EUROPEAN COAST
1535 ARRIVE BASE

```
                          S E C R E T        * CAMERA AND BOMBSIGHT
95 "A" LEAD SQ.
                             HAMILTON *
                             8144 L-O
         WALTER            NELSON       GETCHIUS *        DILLON *
         8826 A-J         8269 I-K      8942 I-Y         9052 I-S
YOUNG         L'ECUYER              PALMER           SEABURG       CRAWFORD
8741 A-M      6946 A-F             7783 I-R          6902 I-G       8255 I-A
                        CALICURA         FABINIAK
                        6838 I-E         7204 I-B
-----------------------------------------------------------------------------
95 "B" HIGH SQ.                 SAVAGE *
                                8745 N-Z
         100th            WELLS          RYAN *         ROSENWEIG *
                         8776 N-B       8657 N-V         8996 N-T
100th        100th               100th          CUMMINGS       SCHULZ
                                                8640 N-D       9152 N-P
                        100th            100th        JUDY
                                                     8438 N-R
-----------------------------------------------------------------------------
95 "C" LOW SQ.                  BROWN *
                                8364 I-W
         BURNS            GROSS          ROSE *         LENNOX *
         8469 L-U        8584 L-A       9037 L-T        8106 L-E
BEARD        TRBOVICH              SALVO            COLEMAN       JACKMAN
8990 A-X     8140 A-C             9177 A-Y          8331 A-G       7194 I-O
         SCHARAR          GIBSON          MILLSPAUGH
         6801 A-A        2447 L-H         6475 L-L
-----------------------------------------------------------------------------
R/T COLLECTIVE CALLSIGNS AND FLARE COLORS:
                     "A" SQ.                "B" SQ.             "C" SQ.
13A 100th FIREBALL LEADER-YY   FIREBALL DOG HI---YY  FIREBALL DOG LO---YY
13B  95th FIREBALL BAKER--RR   FIREBALL BAKER HI-RR  FIREBALL BAKER LO-RR
13C 390th FIREBALL JIG----GG   FIREBALL JIG HI---GG  FIREBALL JIG LO---GG
-----------------------------------------------------------------------------
SHIPS TO MONITOR:          "A" SQ.           "B" SQ.        "C" SQ.
  CHANNEL B              SEABURG I-G       CUMMINGS N-D   COLEMAN A-G
  CHANNEL C 8TH AF       CALICURA I-E      100th          GIBSON L-H
  CHANNEL C 66TH FWG     L'ECUYER A-F
  COMMAND #2 (5295)      YOUNG A-M         100th          BEARD A-X
  M/F D/F                YOUNG A-M         100th          SCHARRAR A-A
  CONTROL POINTS:        GETCHIUS I-Y
                         CRAWFORD I-A
  STRIKE MESSAGES:       GETCHIUS I-Y      SAVAGE N-Z     BROWN I-W
                         CRAWFORD I-A      RYAN N-V       ROSE L-T
                                           SCHULZ N-P     JACKMAN I-O
-----------------------------------------------------------------------------
         LEADERS "A" SQ.  "B" SQ.  "C" SQ.   EXTRA AIRCRAFT:
READINESS         0735     0725     0745     PFF-----0840 A-N
STATIONS          0835     0825     0845     WING----7145 N-F
TAXI      0830    0850     0840     0900
TAKE-OFF  0840    0900     0850     0910
RENDEZVOUS        1030     1025     1035     LAST TAKE-OFF TIME 0955
OVER              BASE     BASE     BASE     ZERO HOUR  1100
     AT         17,000'  18,000'  16,000'
BOMB ALT. (TRUE) 24,000'  24,500'  23,500'
-----------------------------------------------------------------------------
MINIMUM BOMBING ALTITUDES        23,000 VISUAL
                                 20,000 BLIND
```

```
VHF AUTHENTICATOR--MUSIC                    COLORS OF THE DAY
DIVISION RECALL--THE RADIO SHOW
WING RECALL--P.X. RATIONS        0100-0700  GRR  V-VICTOR  Z-ZEBRA
INDIVIDUAL ABORTION--HUNCHBACK FROM 0700-1300 GRR N-NAN    J-JIG
           NECKING DAMES         1300-1900  RGG  O-OBOE    B-BAKER
REFERENCE BASE ALTITUDE--10,000'
REFERENCE BASE WIND---360 Degrees
               50 Knots                  KODAK AUTHENTICATOR
                                           BAKER    86
VHF CALLSIGNS:                             CHARLIE  30
  BOMBERS---VINEGROVE TWO NINE             WILLIE   18
  FIGHTERS--BALANCE 2                      TOMMY    40
  GROUND---66TH FTR WG--OIKSKIN            JASON    22
           8TH AF-------COLGATE            RONALD   03
           3RD DIV------ARROWSMITH         FREDDIE  74
           13 CBW-------RANDOLPH           KARLO    92
                                           GEORGE   48
                                           MICKEY   95
SCOUTING FORCE
  KODAK CONTROL - 2 P-51's MARSHALLING.
  KODAK WHITE - 2 P-51's TO SCOUT W/C TO 0700E.
  KODAK RED - 8 P-51's TO GIVE TGT W/X 20
            MIN. PRIOR TO TGT. TIME.
            IP    "5"   TGT   "6"
  DROWSEY "E" EASY - WILL SCOUT BASE W/X AT
            ASS. ALT ONE HOUR PRIOR TO TAKE-OFF.
  DROWSEY "G" GEORGE - WILL PRECEDE BOMBER STREAM
            BY ONE HOUR.
                                  GEOGRAPHICAL CHECK POINTS
EMERGENCY AIRFIELDS:
  EXTREME EMERGENCY  ST. TROND  A-92 (5047-0511)  G - ZWOLLE
  EMERGENCY          MERVILLE B-53 (5037-0239)    O - DUMMER LAKE
                                                  S - KASSEL
                                                  P - GIESEN
FIGHTER SUPPORT:                                  E - COLOGNE
  (B) 339A AND B GRPS, CALL SIGNS BALANCE TWO-THREE  L - HAMM
      AND TWO-FOUR, R/V 5244-0438 WITH 45 WING AND
      13A, B GRPS., AND COVER SIX CHAFF A/C.

                                  CONTROL POINTS:

                                  1. SOUTHWOLD
                                  2. 5422-0438
                                  3. 5005-0600 (OUT)


PROCEDURE TO FOLLOW WHEN LANDING ON THE CONTINENT:

1. Whenever possible, land at a field at which 8th AF Service Command
Center facilities are located.
2. Have radio operator contact base giving necessary information. Pilot
can contact ground station on VHF.
3. After landing, pilot will (a) arrange for medical assistance, if
necessary, (b) fill out "Forced Landing Card" from rear of pilot's or
co-pilot's seat, (c) safeguard all secret and confidential items on
ship, (d) contact nearest 8th AF Service Command Service Center
representative if one isn't on the field and (e) contact home base.
(Use VHF or W/T in the air or on the ground.)
4. Crew members will be responsible for individual flying equipment.
```

<<<< EXPLANATION - PILOT'S INFORMATION SHEET

- THE ENEMY MONITORED OUR RADIO FREQUENCIES AND WOULD OFTEN ATTEMPT TO INTERFERE BY TRANSMITTING FICTITIOUS MESSAGES. SUCH AS "THIRD AIR DIVISION RETURN TO YOUR BASES." IF THAT OCCURRED, A RESPONSE WOULD REQUEST THE AUTHENTICATOR.. IF THE MESSAGE WAS NOT REPEATED WITH THE WORDS "RADIO SHOW" THE ORDER WOULD BE KNOWN TO BE FALSE. THE AUTHENTICATORS WERE USED ONLY ONCE.

- THE COLORS OF THE DAY WERE A SIGN-COUNTERSIGN ARRANGEMENT. NOTICE THAT THEY WERE GOOD ONLY FOR SIX HOURS.

- THE REFERENCE BASE ALTITUDE WAS USED TO ADVISE "FRIENDLIES" OF YOUR ALTITUDE. FOR EXAMPLE, IF YOU WERE AT 19.000 FEET AND WANTED TO LET YOUR ESCORT KNOW WHERE YOU WERE, YOU WOULD GIVE YOUR ALTITUDE AS "ANGELS 9" — 9,000 FEET ABOVE 10,000 FEET. IF YOU WERE AT 7,000 FEET THE MESSAGE WOULD BE "DEVILS 3".

- IN A SIMILAR FASHION THE BASE WIND WAS USED TO TRANSMIT WIND DATA.

- THE VHF CALL SIGNS WERE USED FOR CALLING BETWEEN THE VARIOUS ORGANIZATIONS. FOR EXAMPLE, IF THE 13TH COMBAT WING LEADER WANTED TO CONTACT HIS HEADQUARTERS, HIS TRANSMISSION WOULD START WITH "ARROWSMITH, THIS IS VINEGROVE TWO NINE, ..." THE CALL SIGNS WERE NOT CHANGED AS FREQUENTLY AS THE AUTHENTICATORS FOR THE SIMPLE REASON THAT IF A TRANSMISSION WAS SUSPECT, IT COULD BE CHECKED WITH THE DAY'S CODE WORDS.

- JUST AS BACK IN THE "INDIANS vs THE COWBOYS" WARS, THE 8TH AIR FORCE HAD ITS SCOUTS. USUALLY P-51'S, P-38'S OR STRIPPED DOWN B-17'S. AGAIN, TO COUNTERACT ENEMY INTERFERENCE, AUTHENTICATORS WERE WIDELY USED. THESE WERE DIFFERENT FOR EACH MISSION.

- AFTER THE INVASION, EMERGENCY AIRFIELDS WERE ESTABLISHED SO THAT AN AIRCRAFT IN TROUBLE COULD LAND ON THE CONTINENT. THE ALPHANUMERIC SYMBOL IS THE MAP COORDINATES AND THE NUMBERS IN THE PARENTHESIS ARE THE CONTROL TOWER FREQUENCIES.

- GEOGRAPHICAL CHECK POINTS ARE USED TO GIVE YOUR LOCATION. FOR EXAMPLE, IF YOU GOT KNOCKED OUT OF FORMATION AND WANTED SOME "LITTLE FRIENDS" TO ESCORT YOU HOME, YOUR CALL MIGHT GO LIKE THIS: "'BALANCE TWO', THIS 'ABUSH J JIG' WE NEED ESCORT AT 'ANGELS 5, 50 MILES NORTHWEST OF 'S, SUGAR'." THIS WOULD TELL THE FIGHTERS WE WERE AT 15,000 FEET AND 50 MILES NORTHWEST OF KASSEL, GERMANY. OBVIOUSLY, CHECK POINTS WERE DIFFERENT FOR EACH MISSION.

- CONTROL POINT IS THE PLACE ON THE ENGLISH COAST WHERE THE BOMBER STREAM DEPARTED FOR EUROPE. THE RADIO FREQUENCIES ARE FOR THE COMMAND AND LIAISON RADIOS, RESPECTIVELY. COMMAND RADIOS WERE THE VOICE AM RADIOS IN THE COCKPIT; THE LIAISON RADIO (WIRELESS TELEGRAPHY OR MORSE CODE) IN THE RADIO ROOM WAS OPERATED BY THE RADIO OPERATOR.

MARCH 10, 1944
MISSION TO DORTMUND GERMANY

I've used several reference works to put together a few details of this mission.

This was the Eighth Air Force's mission number 877, the 95th's 292nd and my 35th.

Eleven Primary Targets, two Secondary Targets and one Target of Opportunity were bombed. Most of them were railway related. At this stage of the war, the main thrust of the 8th was to stop the transportation of supplies to the front. A total of 5,916,000 pounds of bombs were dropped this day.

For each mission we were usually given a Secondary Target. This was to be attacked if, for some reason such as weather, it was not possible to bomb the Primary Target. Similarly, if neither the Primary nor the Secondary could be hit, we could go after any other target we might see and identify. This was a Target of Opportunity.

The First Air Division put up 457 B-17's, the Second A.D.; 376 B-24's and the Third A.D.; 541 B-17's for a total of 1,374 heavies; however, 27 A/C failed to reach the target. As no A/C were lost to enemy action that day, apparently those which failed to reach the target were kept from doing so because of mechanical or other failures.

Of the thirty-two 95th A/C that took off, thirty-one made it to the target. My left wing man, Young, dropped out due to a mechanical failure. Another airplane in the Group, piloted by Jackman, had to land on the Continent on the way back.

My Group, the 95th Bomb Group (H), was one of the three groups in the 13th Combat Wing which, in turn, was a part of the

Third Air Division. The 100th and the 390th were the other groups in the 13th Combat Wing.

On this day the 13th Combat Wing's target was the railway marshalling yards at Dortmund. Dortmund is located in what is generally called the Ruhr Valley. The 13th Combat Wing's strength of 109 A/C was composed of 32 A/C from the 95th and a total of 77 A/C from the 100th and 390th Groups. Individual A/C bomb load consisted of fourteen 500 pound GP bombs for a total of 7,000 pounds.

All of the other targets for this day were in this general area.

To support the heavies, the 8th Air Force put up 644 fighters, 144 P-47's and 500 P-51's. Two enemy A/C were shot down. Three P-51's were lost. Two of the P-51's were shot down by U.S. anti-aircraft guns near the Remagen Bridge. The pilots were MIA. The third P-51 came too close to a formation of B-17's and got himself shot down. He bailed out over Belgium and landed o.k.

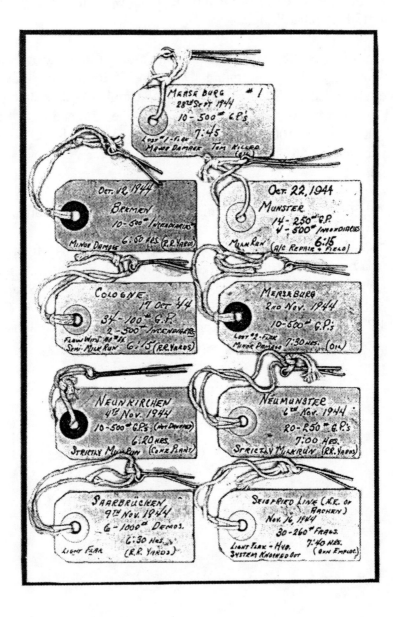

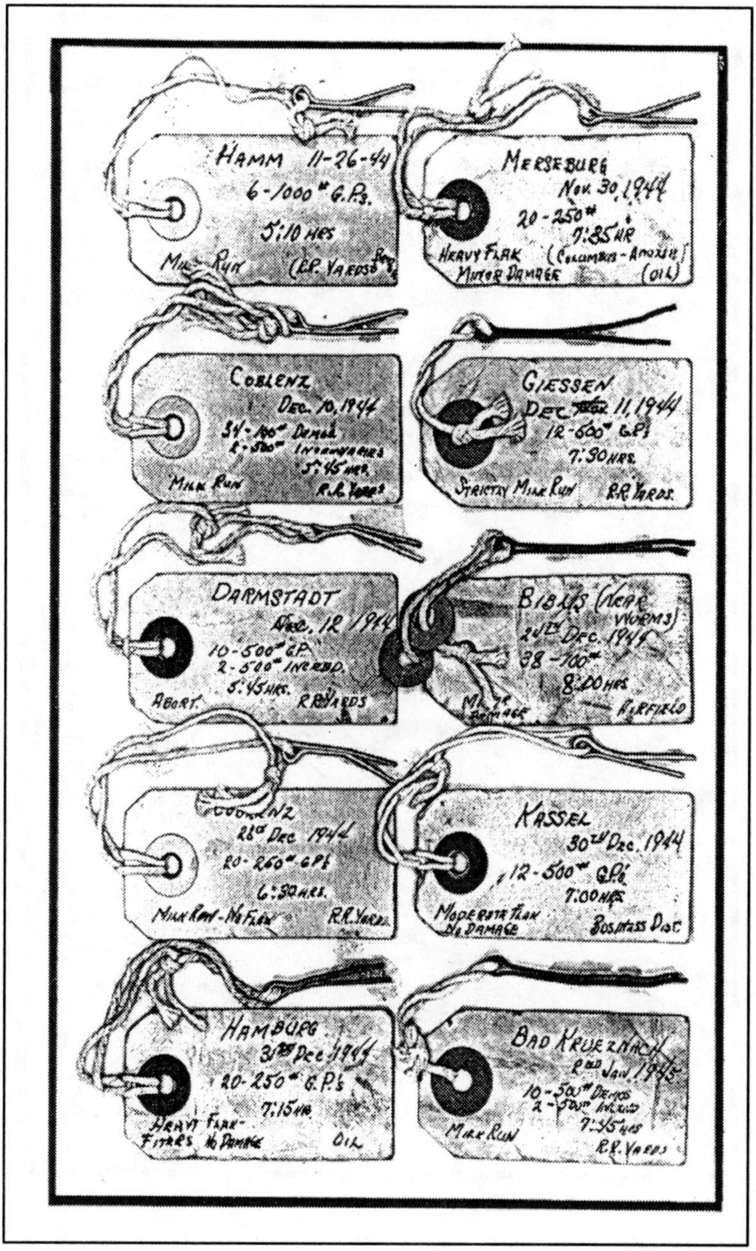
HAMM 11-26-44
6-1000# G.P.s.
5:10 HRS
(R.R. YARDS)
MERSEBURG
Nov. 30, 1944
20-250#
7:35 HR
HEAVY FLAK
MINOR DAMAGE
(OIL)
COBLENZ
DEC. 10, 1944
MILK RUN
R.R. YARDS
GIESSEN
DEC 11, 1944
12-500# G.P.s
7:30 HRS.
STRICTLY MILK RUN
R.R. YARDS
DARMSTADT
DEC. 12 1944
10-500# G.P.
2-500# INCEND.
5:45 HRS.
ABORT.
KASSEL
30th DEC. 1944
12-500# G.P.s
7:00 HRS
MODERATE FLAK
NO DAMAGE
HAMBURG
31st DEC 1944
20-250# G.P.s
7:15 HR
HEAVY FLAK
OIL
BAD KRUEZNACH
2nd JAN 1945
MILK RUN
R.R. YARDS

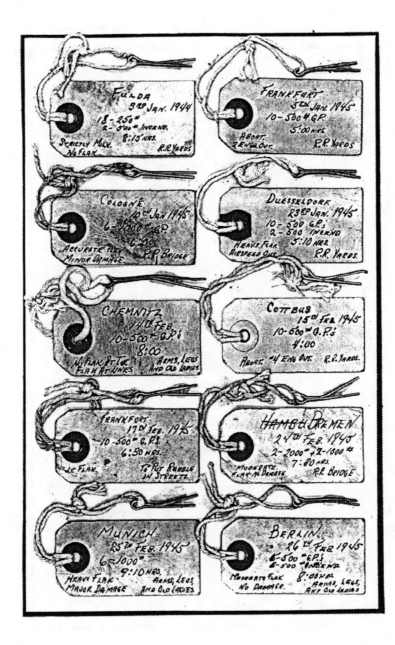

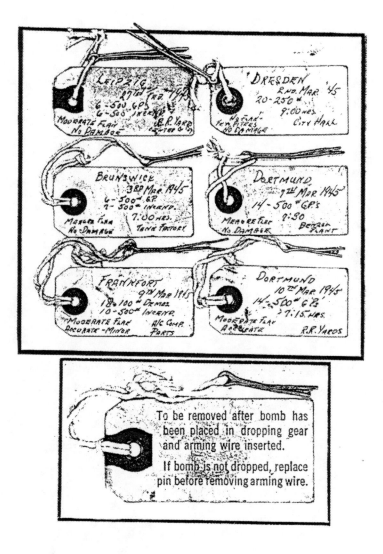

THE IMPORTANT SIDE OF THE BOMB TAG
FULL SIZE

ABOUT THE AUTHOR

Written by John C. Walter, this book recounts his military experiences during World War II from his 1942 enlistment in the United States Army Air Force as an Aviation Cadet to service as pilot-in-command of a B-17 Flying Fortress with the 95th Bomb Group of the 8th Air Force in Europe. After graduation from the University of Southern California School of Engineering, he joined Cummins Engine Company. During his career with Cummins, he wrote a number of technical papers which were published both in the U.S. and England. For a number of years he was Chairman of Cummins Technical Publication Policy Committee.